STAGE START

20 Plays for Children
(Ages 3-12)

First published in 2013 by
JemBooks
Cork,
Ireland
www.drama-in-ecce.com

ISBN: 978-0-9568966-2-9

Typesetting by Gough Typesetting Service, Dublin

STAGE START

20 PLAYS FOR CHILDREN
(AGES 3-12)

Julie Meighan

JemBooks

About the Author

Julie Meighan is a lecturer in Drama in Education at the Cork Institute of Technology. She has taught Drama to all age groups and levels. She is the author of the Amazon bestselling *Drama Start: Drama Activities, Plays and Monologues for Young Children (Ages 3 -8)*. ISBN 978-0956896605 and *Drama Start Two: Drama Activities and Plays for Children (Ages 9 -12)*. *ISBN 978-0-9568966-1-2.*

Contents

Introduction

I have taught Drama to children for the last eighteen years. The following is a selection of plays that I have written and that have been performed on numerous occasions with different Drama Groups I have worked with throughout the years. The first nine plays - The Lion and the Mouse, The Little Red Hen, The Gingerbread Man, The Ants and the Grasshopper, The Enormous Turnip, Chicken Licken, The Hare and the Tortoise, The Three Billy Goats Gruff, The Ugly Duckling and The Boy Who Cried Wolf - are all based on well-known and well-loved, traditional children's stories.

The play Chinese New Year is based on the legend of how each animal became associated with a Chinese year. The Lonely Dragon is based on a therapeutic story I wrote about isolation and making friends. How the Zebra got his Stripes tells the fun story of the legend of how all the different jungle animals came to look like they do today. The Selfish Giant is based on the very popular short story by Oscar Wilde; The Land of Trolls and Gargoyles is a play about a child's attachment to his parent, and No Excuse deals with the topic of bullying. Caught in the Act, At Doctor's Crowne and A Winter's Tale have fewer characters and can be used in a small drama class or with smaller groups. Finally, Anne of Green Gables is a duologue based on the very famous book Anne of Green Gables by L. M. Montgomery. In the scene, Anne accidentally gets Diana drunk and chaos ensues.

Each play is between five minutes and twenty minutes long. The play can be adapted to suit the various needs of the class/group. The first eight plays use a lot of repetition so it is very easy for young children to learn their lines. The cast list is flexible – more characters can be added and existing characters can be changed or omitted. Most of the characters can be on stage throughout the play, with children walking to the centre of the stage when it is time to say their lines. In the earlier plays the teacher/leader can assume the role of the storyteller if the children can't read or are not at the reading level required.

The costumes for all the plays are or can be very simple. For example, the children can just wear something in the colour of their animal, wear a mask or use some face paint. A word of advice: if the children wear masks, make sure they don't cover their mouths as it would make it difficult to hear them speak. The rest of the plays also have a flexible cast list as more characters can be added and existing characters can be changed or omitted easily depending on the requirement of the group. All suggestions for stage directions are included in brackets and italics.

I hope you enjoy performing the following plays as much as my drama groups have over the years.

Good Luck!

The Lion and the Mouse

Characters: Three Storytellers, Lion, Mouse, Elephants, Giraffes, Snakes, Owls. You can have as many elephants, giraffes, snakes and owls as you want.

(Stage Directions: all the animals are in a semi-circle on the stage; they are grouped according to their animal type. Storytellers can be placed on the right or the left of the stage.)

Storyteller 1: One hot day a lion was asleep in a cave. *(Lion is sleeping in the centre of the stage.)*

Storyteller 2: Suddenly a little mouse ran over his paw. *(Mouse comes scampering out quickly and touches the Lion's paw.)*

Storyteller 3: The lion woke up with a loud roar. He grabbed the mouse with his paw and said ... *(Lion wakes up and grabs the mouse.)*

Lion: I'm going to kill you and eat you up. *(Lion roars loudly.)*

Mouse: Squeak, Squeak! Please, Mr. Lion, Please don't eat me. Some day I will help you.

Lion: Ha, Ha, Ha! You, help me! Don't make me laugh, but I'm not that hungry so I will let you go. *(Lion pushes the mouse away.)*

Storyteller 1: The lion laughed and laughed and the mouse ran home.

Storyteller 2: A few days later the lion was out in the jungle.

Lion: I think I will scare my friends. I am very scary because I'm King of the Jungle. *(He goes to each group of animals and roars at them. All the animals are scared and move away from him.)*

Storyteller 3: Suddenly the lion got caught in a trap and said... *(He is in the centre of stage when he falls to his knees.)*

Lion: Oh dear, how will I get out of here? *(Lion looks around the stage desperately.)*

Storyteller 1: After a while he heard some elephants. *(Elephants move from the semi-circle and they circle the lion. They must make sure the audience can see their faces.)*

Lion: Elephants, elephants, please help me.

Elephants: Oh No! We will not help you. *(Elephants trundle off back to the other animals.)*

Storyteller 2: Then a few giraffes passed by. He cried … *(Giraffes leave the semi-circle and move behind the lion.)*

Lion: Giraffes, Giraffes, please help me. *(Lion looks up at the giraffes.)*

Giraffes: Oh no, we will not help you. *(Giraffes go back to their place in the semi-circle.)*

Storyteller 3: The lion grew cold and hungry *(the lion shivers and rubs his stomach)* and began to think he would never get home to his nice, warm cave. Then he heard the hissing of snakes. *(Snakes moves towards the centre of the stage near the lion.)*

Lion: Snakes, snakes, please help me. *(The lion looks up at the snakes.)*

Snakes: Sssssssss, oh no we will not help you, sssssssssssssssss. *(Snakes go back to the semi-circle.)*

Storyteller 1: As night came the lion began to cry.

Lion: Boo hoo, I am stuck in this trap and none of my friends will help me.

Storyteller 2: Then he heard some owls hooting in the trees. *(Owls move centre stage, towards the lion.)*

Lion: Owls, Owls, please help me. *(Lion looks up at the owls.)*

Owls: Tu Whit, Tu Whoo, we will not help youuuuuuuuuuu. *(Owls go back to the semi-circle.)*

Storyteller 3: The lion was very sad. *(Lion starts crying.)* He didn't know what to do. Then he heard the squeaking of a mouse.

Mouse: Squeak, squeak! Why are you crying Mr. Lion? *(Mouse comes from behind the other animals.)*

Lion: I'm stuck in this trap and nobody will help me.

Mouse: I will help you.

Storyteller 1: The mouse began to bite through the rope and at last the lion was free.

Lion: I'm free, I'm free! I never thought you could help me because you are too small.

Storyteller 2: From then on the lion and the mouse were very good friends.

Storyteller 3: The lesson of the story is…

Storyteller 1: …bigger is not always better!

(Mouse and Lion hug.)

The Little Red Hen

Characters: Six storytellers, the Little Red Hen, dog 1, dogs, cat 1, cats, goose 1, geese, duck 1, ducks (*you can have as many dogs, cats, ducks and geese as you want*)**, farmer and miller.**

(Stage Directions: Storytellers are on the left-side of the stage and the animals are all in a semi-circle in the centre of the stage.)

Storyteller 1: Once upon a time there was a little red hen that lived on a farm.

Storyteller 2: She was always busy! *(She moves around the stage looking busy.)*

Storyteller 3: She spent all morning laying eggs for the farmer. (*The Little Red Hen bends down and lays eggs. Balloons can be used for the eggs.*)

Farmer: Chick Chicken! Please lay an egg for my tea. *(The Farmer comes centre stage and talks to the Little Red Hen.)*

All Sing: Chick, Chick, Chick, Chicken,
Chick, chick, chick, chick, chicken,
Lay a little egg for me!
Chick, chick, chick, chick, chicken,
I want one for my tea!
I haven't had an egg since Easter
And now it's half past three!
So chick, chick, chick, chick, chicken
Lay a little egg for me!

Storyteller 4: After the Little Red Hen laid her egg…..

Storyteller 5: …..she found a grain of wheat.

Storyteller 6: She wanted to plant it in a field.

Red Hen: I think I'll ask my animal friends to help me. *(She moves towards the dogs.)* Dogs, Dogs! Will you help me plant the wheat?

Dogs: Oh no, we will not help you. We are too busy burying our bones. *(They all make burying actions.)*

Dog 1: Get the ducks to help you. *(They all point to the ducks.)*

Red Hen: Ducks, Ducks! Will you help me plant the wheat? *(Little Red Hen moves towards the ducks.)*

Ducks: Oh no, we will not help you. We are too busy swimming. (*They all make swimming actions.*)

Duck 1: Get the geese to help you. (*All the ducks point to the geese.*)

Red Hen: Geese, Geese! Will you help me plant the wheat? (*She moves towards the geese.*)

Geese: Oh no, we will not help you. We are too busy sunbathing. (*All the geese are lying on the floor enjoying the sun and rubbing lotion on themselves.*)

Goose 1: Get the cats to help you. (*All geese point towards the cats.*)

Red Hen: Cats, Cats! Will you help me plant the wheat?

Cats: Oh no, we will not help you. We are too busy washing our paws. (*Cats wash their paws.*)

Cat 1: Plant it yourself.

Storyteller 6: No one would help the little, red hen so she planted it herself. (*Red Hen, centre stage, mimes planting the wheat.*)

Storyteller 1: The sun and the rain helped the wheat to grow.

Storyteller 2: Soon the wheat was tall and yellow and needed to be cut.

Red Hen: I think I'll ask my animal friends to help me. Dogs, Dogs! Will you help me cut the wheat? (*She moves towards the dogs.*)

Dogs: Oh no, we will not help you. We are too busy burying our bones. (*The dogs mime burying their bones.*)

Dog 1: Get the ducks to help you. (*Dogs point at the ducks.*)

Red Hen: Ducks, Ducks! Will you help me cut the wheat?

Ducks: Oh no, we will not help you. We are too busy swimming.

Duck 1: Get the geese to help you. (*All the ducks point to the geese.*)

Red Hen: Geese, Geese! Will you help me cut the wheat?

Geese: Oh no, we will not help you. We are too busy sunbathing.

Goose 1: Get the cats to help you. (*All geese move (point?) towards the cats.*)

Red Hen: Cats, Cats! Will you help me cut the wheat?

Cats: Oh no, we will not help you. We are too busy washing our faces.

Cat 1: Plant it yourself.

Storyteller 3: So the little red hen cut the wheat herself.

Storyteller 4: So she took the wheat to the miller.

Storyteller 5: The miller turned the wheat into flour.

Miller: *(Gives Little Red Hen the bag of flour.)* Here's your flour to make bread and cakes.

Storyteller 6: The little red hen thanked the miller.

Storyteller 1: She made bread and cakes.

Red Hen: Who will help me eat the bread?

All animals: We will!

Red Hen: Oh no, I will eat it myself. If you want to eat the food what will you do next time?

All: We will share the work.

Storytellers: THE END!

All sing : Chick, Chick, Chick, Chicken.
Chick, chick, chick, chick, chicken,
Lay a little egg for me!
Chick, chick, chick, chick, chicken,
I want one for my tea!
I haven't had an egg since Easter
And now it's half past three!
So chick, chick, chick, chick, chicken
Lay a little egg for me!

The Gingerbread Man

Characters: Gingerbread Man, three storytellers, old woman, old man, cow, horse, dog, two bears and a fox.

(Stage Directions: Three storytellers stand on the left side of the stage. Old woman is sitting on a chair – knitting or reading a book and Old Man is digging up vegetables on the right side of stage. The rest of the animals can be back stage or standing quietly in a semicircle.)

Storyteller 1: Once upon a time, a little, old woman and a little, old man lived in a little, old house. One day, the little, old woman decided to make a Gingerbread Man.

Old Woman: I think I will make gingerbread for the old man's tea. He will love that. *(She gets up from the chair and goes to centre stage. She mimes making the gingerbread and putting it in the oven as Storyteller 2 speaks.)*

Storyteller 2: She cut the Gingerbread Man out of dough. She gave him chocolate drops for eyes and a piece of lemon for his mouth. Then she put him in the oven to bake. After a while she said to herself …

Old Woman: That Gingerbread Man must be ready by now. *(She mimes looking into the oven etc.)*

Storyteller 3: She opened the oven door. UP jumped the Gingerbread Man, and away he ran, out the front door! *(Gingerbread Man jumps out from the oven.)*

Gingerbread Man: Hello, I am the Gingerbread Man.

Old Man: Don't run away. I want you for my tea. *(He puts his hand up to try and stop the Gingerbread Man.)*

Gingerbread Man: Run, run, as fast as you can. You can't catch me I'm the Gingerbread Man!

Storyteller 3: The little, old woman and the little, old man ran, but they couldn't catch the Gingerbread Man. *(They run after him, running around the stage in a circle. Old Man and Old Woman get tired, so they stop.)*

Storyteller 1: The Gingerbread Man ran past the cow grazing in the field. *(Cow comes out onto the stage.)*

Cow: Moo! Moo! Stop! Stop! Gingerbread Man, I want to eat you.

Gingerbread Man: Run, run, as fast as you can. You can't catch me I'm the Gingerbread Man! *(Cow chases him but can't catch him so she stops and either goes back to her original position or…instruction missing?)*

Storyteller 2: The cow ran, but she couldn't catch the Gingerbread Man. Then he met a horse drinking at the well. *(Horse comes out onto the stage.)*

Horse: Neigh! Neigh! Stop! Stop! Gingerbread Man, I want to eat you.

Gingerbread Man: Run, run, as fast as you can. You can't catch me, I'm the Gingerbread Man! *(Horse chases him but can't catch him so he stops.)*

Storyteller 3: The horse ran, but she couldn't catch the Gingerbread Man. Then he met a dog playing in the field. *(Dog comes out onto the stage.)*

Dog: Woof! Woof! Stop! Stop! Gingerbread Man, I want to eat you.

Gingerbread Man: Run, run, as fast as you can. You can't catch me, I'm the Gingerbread Man! *(Dog chases him but he gets tired and stops. Dog is panting.)*

Storyteller 1: He ran between two bears having a picnic.

Bears: Growl! Growl! Stop! Stop! Gingerbread Man, we want to eat you.

Gingerbread Man: Run, run, as fast as you can. You can't catch me, I'm the Gingerbread Man! *(Bears chase the Gingerbread Man but they get tired and have to stop.)*

Storyteller 2: The bears jumped up and ran after him. They ran, and ran, but they couldn't catch that Gingerbread Man!

Storyteller 3: Soon, the Gingerbread Man came to a river and started to cry. *(Gingerbread Man cries and Fox creeps up behind him.)* He saw a fox.

Fox: Why are you crying, Gingerbread Man?

Gingerbread Man: I've run away from an old woman, an old man, a cow, a horse, a dog and two picnicking bears, and I can run away from you!

Fox: If you don't get across this river quickly, the old woman, the old man, the cow, the horse, the dog and the two picnicking bears, will surely catch you. Hop on my tail and I'll carry you across. *(Fox points to his tail.)*

Storyteller 2: The Gingerbread Man saw that he had no time to lose because the old woman, the old man, the cow, the horse, the dog and the two picnicking bears were very close behind him. . He quickly hopped onto the fox's tail. *(Gingerbread Man mimes getting onto the fox's tail. He holds on to his back and fox mimes swimming.)*

Fox: The water's deep, climb up on my back so you won't get wet. Oh! The water's even deeper! Climb up on my head so you won't get wet!

(Gingerbread Man holds onto Fox's back and he jumps in front. Then Fox bends down, so his head is touching Gingerbread Man's back.)

Storyteller 3: And the Gingerbread Man did as the fox told him.

Fox: It's too deep! Climb onto my nose so you won't get wet! *(The gingerbread man's back touches the fox's nose.)*

Storyteller 1: And the Gingerbread Man did that but then, with a flick of his head, the Fox tossed the Gingerbread Man into the air and opened his mouth, but the Gingerbread Man jumped to the other side of the river.

Gingerbread Man: *(to everyone)* Run, run, as fast as you can. You can't catch me, I'm the Gingerbread Man!

(All the other characters are on the other side of the stage/river and they start to cry.)

The Ants and the Grasshopper

Characters: Three storytellers, three ants, grasshopper, owls, squirrels and bears.

(Stage Directions: the owls, squirrels and bears are in a large semicircle stage right; storytellers are stage left and the ants are in the centre of the stage.)

Storyteller 1: One hot summer's day …

Storyteller 2: … there were some ants working hard.

Storyteller 3: They were collecting food for the winter. (*All the ants are miming digging, pulling and pushing.*)

Ant 1: I am so hot.

Ant 2: Me too!

Ant 3: This is very hard work.

Storyteller 1: They saw a grasshopper listening to some music on his iPod. (*Grasshopper passes by, singing and dancing; the ants stop work and look at him.*)

Storyteller 2: He was dancing …

Storyteller 3: … and laughing and enjoying the lovely weather.

Grasshopper: Ants, you are so silly. You need to enjoy the sunshine.

(Ants start working again.)

Ant 1: We are working hard.

Ant 2: We want to have food for the winter. (*Grasshopper keeps dancing.*)

Storyteller 1: The grasshopper continued enjoying himself. (*The Ants keep working and move stage right.*)

Storyteller 2: Winter started to come and the weather got colder and colder.

Storyteller 3: The snow began to fall.

Storyteller 1: The grasshopper was cold and hungry. (*Grasshopper rubs his stomach and shivers. He looks at the owls who start to fly around the stage.*)

Grasshopper: I am cold and hungry; perhaps my friends the owls will feed me. Owls! Owls! Will you please feed me?

Owls: (*Owls fly around the grasshopper and stop centre stage. They stand around the grasshopper.*) Twit Tuhooo! Oh no, we will not feed you. (*They fly back to their place in the semicircle.*)

Grasshopper: Oh dear! I know, I will ask my friends the bears to feed me. (*Grasshopper walks towards the bears.*) Bears! Bears! Please feed me. (*Bears are asleep so he wakes them up and they walk to the centre stage.*)

Bears: (*The bears are very angry that they have been woken up.*) Growl! Growl! Oh no, we will not feed you. (*The bears go back to their place in the semicircle.*)

Storyteller 1: Then the grasshopper saw some squirrels. (*The squirrels mime eating nuts stage right.*)

Grasshopper: Squirrels! Squirrels! Please feed me! (*They squirrels walk towards him.*)

Squirrels: Oh no, we will not feed you. (*They hop back to stage right.*)

Storyteller 2: The grasshopper was very cold and hungry. He didn't know what to do. (*Grasshopper is shivering and rubbing his stomach.*)

Storyteller 3: Then he thought of the ants. (*The ants move to the centre of the stage.*)

Grasshopper: Ants! Ants! Please feed me. (*The ants go into a huddle away from the grasshopper.*)

Storyteller 1: The ants thought about it and decided to give him some food. (*All the ants face the grasshopper.*)

Ant 1: You must promise that next year you will work hard in the summer. (*Grasshopper gets down on his hands and knees.*)

Grasshopper: Oh thank you Ants, I promise.

Storyteller 1: That summer the grasshopper kept his promise and worked hard to collect food for the next winter. (*Grasshopper mimes pushing, pulling, carrying and digging with all the ants.*)

Storyteller 2: The lesson of the story is: fail to prepare ...

Storyteller 3: ...prepare to fail.

The Enormous Turnip

Characters: Three storytellers, old man, old woman, boy, girl, dog, cat and mouse.

(Stage Directions: storytellers on stage left and the old man in the centre. All the other characters are in a line off-stage or they can be on-stage, with each character miming doing their own thing.)

Storyteller 1: Once upon a time there lived a little old man.

Storyteller 2: One day he planted a turnip seed in his garden. *(Old man plants his seed.)*

Old Man: This turnip is going to be very big and very sweet. *(Looks at the audience.)*

Storyteller 3: The turnip grew and grew.

Old Man: I think it is time to dig up the turnip. *(Old man mimes trying to pull it up.)*

Storyteller 1: He pulled and pulled but he couldn't pull up the turnip.

Old Man: I know, I will ask my wife to help me. Wife! Wife! Please help me to pull up the turnip. *(Wife holds on to him at the waist and they try pulling up the turnip.)*

Storyteller 2: His wife came and helped him.

Storyteller 3: They pulled and pulled but they couldn't pull up the turnip.

Wife: I know, I will ask the boy to help us. Boy! Boy! Please help us to pull up the turnip. *(She calls for the boy and the boy comes to help them.)*

Storyteller 1: The boy came and helped them. *(The boy holds on to her at the waist.)*

Storyteller 2: They pulled and pulled but they couldn't pull up the turnip.

Boy: I know I will ask the girl to help us. Girl! Girl! Please help us to pull up the turnip. *(He calls for the girl and the girl comes to help them.)*

Storyteller 3: The girl came and helped them. *(The girl holds on to him at the waist.)*

Storyteller 1: They pulled and pulled but they couldn't pull up the turnip.

Girl: I know, I will ask the dog to help us. Dog! Dog! Please help us to pull up the turnip. (*She calls for the dog and the dog comes to help her.*)

Storyteller 2: The dog came and helped them. (*The dog holds on to her at the waist.*)

Storyteller 3: They pulled and pulled but they couldn't pull up the turnip.

Dog: I know, I will ask the cat to help us. Cat! Cat! Please help us to pull up the turnip. (*He calls for the cat and the cat comes to help them.*)

Storyteller 1: The cat came and helped them. (*The cat holds on to him at the waist.*)

Storyteller 2: They pulled and pulled but they couldn't pull up the turnip.

Cat: I know, I will ask the mouse to help us. Mouse! Mouse! Please help us to pull up the turnip. (*She calls for the mouse and the mouse comes to help them.*)

Storyteller 3: The mouse came and helped them. (*The mouse holds onto her at the waist.*)

Storyteller 1: They pulled and pulled and then suddenly they pulled up the turnip. (*They all fall over.*)

Storyteller 2: Everyone was very happy and they all thanked the mouse. (*Everyone shakes hands with the mouse.*)

Storyteller 3: Everyone had turnip soup for dinner. (*The wife mimes giving each one of them a bowl of soup and they mime drinking it.*)

Chicken Licken

Characters: Three storytellers, Chicken-Licken, Cockey-Lockey, Ducky-Lucky, Goosey-Loosey, Turkey-Lurkey and Foxy-Loxy.

(Stage Directions: Chicken-Licken is moving around the centre stage, miming picking up corn. All the other animals are either off stage or on the stage miming doing different things. Storytellers are stage left.)

Storyteller 1: One summer's day, Chicken-Licken was busy picking up corn in the barnyard. *(Chicken Licken is moving around the stage, miming picking up corn.)*

Storyteller 2: When all of a sudden an acorn from the big oak tree fell down and hit her right on the top of her head – kerrrr flop.

Storyteller 3: She got a terrible fright.

Chicken-Licken: Oh! The sky is falling! The sky is falling! I am going to tell the king!

Storyteller 1: And away she went, to tell the king the sky is falling down. After a while she came to Cockey-Lockey. *(Cockey-Lockey walks towards Chicken-Licken who is in the centre of the stage.)*

Cockey-Lockey: Where are you going, Chicken-Licken?

Chicken-Licken: Oh, Cockey-Lockey. The sky is falling! I am going to tell the king.

Cockey-Lockey: I will go with you! *(They walk in a circle around the stage and they come back to the centre stage where they see Ducky-Lucky.)*

Storyteller 2: They went on and on and on. After a time, they met Ducky-Lucky.

Ducky-Lucky: Where are you going, Chicken-Licken and Cockey-Lockey?

Chicken-Licken/Cockey-Lockey: Oh, Ducky-Lucky! The sky is falling! We are going to tell the king!

Ducky-Lucky: Wait! I will go with you. *(They walk in a circle around the stage and they come back to the centre stage where they see Goosey-Loosey.)*

Storyteller 3: And they hurried off. They went on and on and on! Soon they came to Goosey-Loosey.

Goosey: Hey, where are you two going?

Chicken/Cockey/Ducky: Oh, Goosey-Loosey! The sky is falling! We are going to tell the king.

Goosey: Then I will go with you! (*They walk in a circle around the stage and they come back to the centre stage where they meet Turkey-Lurkey.*)

Storyteller 3: Before long they came to Turkey-Lurkey.

Turkey: Where are you all going in such a rush?

All: Oh, Turkey-Lurkey. The sky is falling! We are going to tell the king.

Turkey: Well, hey, wait for me! I will go with you. (*They walk in a circle around the stage and they come back to the centre stage where they see the fox.*)

Storyteller 1: They went on and on and on. After a while they came to Foxy-Loxy.

Foxy: Say, where are you all going?

All: Foxy-Loxy! Foxy-Loxy! The sky is falling! We are going to tell the king.

Foxy: Well, I know a short cut to the king's palace. Follow me.

Turkey: Oh, great! He knows a short cut to the king's palace!

Storytellers: They went on and on and on. Then they came to Foxy-Loxy's house. (*They all follow Foxy-Loxy, walking in a straight line.*)

Foxy: This is the short cut to the palace. I'll go in first and then you follow me, one-by-one. (*One-by-one they go into the den. The den can be off-stage in the front or behind stage.*)

Storytellers: In went Turkey-Lurkey. Sssssnap! Off went Turkey-Lurkey's head. In went Goosey-Loosey. Kerrrr-POP! Off went Goosey-Loosey's head. In went Ducky-Lucky. Kerrrr-unch! Off went Ducky-Lucky's head. In went Cocky-Lockey. (*Chicken-Licken looks into the den and sees what is happening.*)

Cockey: (*Excitedly*) Go Home, Chicken-Licken! Go Home!

Storyteller 1: Can you guess what happened next? (*pause*) Kerrrrr-Aaaack! Off went Cockey-Lockey's head.

Storyteller 2: Chicken-Licken ran home. (*Chicken-Licken runs really fast around the stage, looking scared.*) She did not tell the king that the sky was falling.

Storyteller 3: And since that day the others have never been seen again. And the poor king has never been told that the sky is falling down!

The Hare and the Tortoise

Characters: 3 storytellers, hare, tortoise, foxes, badgers, hedgehogs, bears and an eagle.

(Stage Directions: The three storytellers are on the left hand side of the stage and the tortoise is moving around the stage in slow motion.).

Storyteller 1: Once upon a time there lived a tortoise.

Storyteller: 2: He liked to go for a leisurely stroll by the edge of a big forest.

Storyteller 3: One day a hare came bounding up towards him. *(Hare comes running on the stage.)*

Hare: *(He pushes the tortoise out of the way and nearly knocks him over.)* Out of my way you slow coach. You must be so bored because it takes you so long to get anywhere.

Storyteller 1: The tortoise looked up at the hare and said…

Tortoise: I know I could beat you in a race any day.

Hare: You beat me? Don't make me laugh! I am so much faster than you. *(He shows off his muscles and starts to run up and down.)*

Storyteller 2: The hare laughed and laughed

Storyteller 3: Then he met some foxes. *(Foxes enter the centre of the stage.)*

Hare: Foxes, do you think that tortoise could beat me in a race?

Foxes: Oh, no he couldn't. *(Foxes shake their heads in disbelief.)*

Tortoise: Oh yes, I could. *(He nods his head.)*

Storyteller 1: Then some hedgehogs came to see what was happening. *(Hedgehogs enter the centre of the stage.)*

Hare: Hedgehogs, do you think that tortoise could beat me in a race?

Hedgehogs: Oh yes, he could. *(The Hedgehogs nod their heads.)*

Hare: Oh no, he couldn't. *(He shakes his head.)*

Storyteller 2: The badgers that were underground heard the arguing and came up to the surface. *(They mime moving to the earth and getting to the surface.)*

Badgers: What's going on here? *(They are annoyed that they have been disturbed by the noise.)*

Hare: The tortoise thinks that he can beat me in a race. What do you think?

Badgers: Oh no, he couldn't. *(Badgers shake their heads.)*

Tortoise: Oh yes, I could. *(He nods his head.)*

Storyteller 3: The bears that were sleeping heard the noise and came trundling along. *(Bears enter the centre stage by making bear noise and taking big loud steps.)*

Bears: What's going on here?

Hare: The silly tortoise thinks he can be beat me in a race. What do you think?

Bears: Oh yes, he could. *(They shake their heads.)*

Storyteller 1: The animals continued to argue about who would win the race. *(All the animals start arguing with one another making lots of noise.)*

Storyteller 2: Then, suddenly the eagle swooped down to where all the animals were. *(Eagle comes flying gracefully on to the stage.)*

Eagle: *(Eagle uses a whistle to stop the noise.)* What's going on here?

Hare: The silly tortoise thinks he can beat me in a race. Do you think he could beat me?

Eagle: I don't know but there is one way of finding out. Why don't you have a race?

Everyone: What a great idea. *(They all start cheering.)*

Eagle: Right: Hare and Tortoise line up at the starting line. *(The hare and the tortoise start limbering up and they get ready at the start line.)* On your marks, get set, GO!

Storyteller 3: All the animals cheered at the side as the hare ran off very quickly and the tortoise just plodded along.

Storyteller 1: After a while the hare stopped and said…

Hare: *(He wipes his brow.)* I'm already half way through so I think I will have a nap in the warm sunshine. *(The hare starts to make himself comfortable, lies down and starts snoring.)*

Storyteller 2: The hare fell fast asleep and the tortoise walked steadily on and on.

Storyteller 3: The hare woke up suddenly. (*He starts to yawn and stretch.*)

Hare: What a nice sleep. No sign of the tortoise so I better stroll along and finish the race.

Storyteller 1: The hare ran to the finish line.

Storyteller 2: Just as he got there he saw the tortoise crossing the line.

Storyteller 3: All the other animals were cheering and celebrating the tortoise's victory. (*All the other animals start to congratulate the tortoise. The hare stomps off in anger.*)

All storytellers: The lesson of the story is …..

Tortoise: Slow and steady wins the race.

Everyone: (*Except the hare who is sulking.*) Hip, Hip, Hooray! Hip, Hip, Hooray, Hip, Hip, Hooray!!!!!!!!!!!!!

The Three Billy Goats Gruff

Characters: Three storyteller, the Smallest Billy Goat, the Middle-Sized Billy Goat and the Biggest Billy Goat and the Troll.

(Stage directions: The three billy goats are happily playing with each other and the three storytellers are on the left side of the stage.)

Storyteller 1: Once upon a time there lived three billy goats gruff.

Storyteller 2: They spent every winter in a barn that kept them nice and warm.

Storyteller 3: But when the summer came they like to trippety trip over the bridge to the beautiful green meadow on the other side of the river.

Smallest Billy Goat: I'm really hungry. I think I will cross the bridge to eat some lovely green grass in the meadow.

Storyteller 1: What the billy goats didn't know was that under the bridge there lived a really ugly troll.

Storyteller 2: The troll was nasty and horrible.

Storyteller 3: Nobody crossed the Bridge without the troll's permission and he never gave permission.

Smallest Billy Goat: I can't wait to get to the meadow. *(He goes trippety trip on the bridge but half way over out pops the troll.)*

Troll: Who is that trippety tripping over my bridge?

Smallest Billy Goat: Oh, it's only me. Please let me pass. I only want to go to the meadow to eat some sweet grass.

Troll: Oh no, you are not. I'm going to eat you.

Smallest Billy Goat: Oh, no, please, Mr. Troll, I'm only the smallest Billy Goat Gruff. I'm much too tiny for you to eat, and I wouldn't taste very good. Why don t you wait for my brother, the middle-sized Billy Goat? He is much bigger than I am and would be much more tasty.

Troll: Well, I suppose I could wait.

Middle-Sized Billy Goat: I think I will join my brother on the meadow and eat some lovely lush grass. *(He goes trippety trip on the bridge but half way over out pops the troll.)*

Troll: Who is that trippety tripping over my bridge?

Smallest Billy Goat: Oh it's only me. Please let me pass. I only want to go to the meadow to eat some sweet grass.

Troll: Oh no, you are not. I'm going to eat you.

Middle-Sized Billy Goat: Oh, no, please, Mr. Troll, I m only the middle-sized Billy Goat Gruff. I'm much too tiny for you to eat, and I wouldn't taste very good. Why don t you wait for my brother, the third Billy Goat? He is much bigger than I am and would be tastier than me.

Troll: Well, I suppose I could wait.

Biggest Billy Goat: I am all alone here I think I will join my brothers in the meadow and get some nice sweet grass to eat.

(He goes trippety trip on the bridge but half way over out pops the troll.)

Troll: Who is that trippety tripping over my bridge?

Biggest Billy Goat: Oh it only me. Please let me pass. I only want to go to the meadow to eat some sweet grass.

Troll: Oh no, you are not. I'm going to eat you.

Biggest Billy Goat: That's what you think!

Storyteller 1: He lowered his horns, galloped along the bridge and butted the ugly troll. Up, up, up, went the troll into the air...

Storyteller 2: then down, down, down into the rushing river below. He disappeared below the swirling waters.

Biggest Billy Goat: That taught him a lesson.

Storyteller 3: He continued across the bridge and met with his brothers and they ate grass and played for the rest of summer. *(The three Billy Goats are playing with each other.)*

The Ugly Duckling

Characters: Three storytellers, the Ugly Duckling, Mother Duck, Old Duck, ducklings, four ducks, turkey, red hen, chickens, two dogs, two wild ducks, tom cat, two children.

(Stage directions: Storytellers on the left hand side of the stage and the mother duck in the centre sitting on her eggs. Eggs could be painted balloons that burst as soon as the eggs crack.)

Storyteller 1: There was once duck who lived near a deep river.

Storyteller 2: The duck was sitting on her eggs in her nest……

Storyteller 3: …..waiting for the eggs to hatch.

Storyteller 1: She had been there a long time.

Storyteller 2: She was starting to get bored.

Mother Duck: I have been sitting on my eggs for such a long time. *(Mother Duck sighs loudly.)*

Storyteller 1: Suddenly, she heard a noise. *(Children can make a cracking noise from behind or off stage.)*

Mother Duck: What was that? Oh my goodness, the eggs are beginning to hatch at last. *(She looks at the eggs with a shocked look on her face.)*

Storyteller 2: One shell cracked, then another. *(Cracking noises come from off stage and then each duck lifts their head and say peep, peep and quack, quack.)*

Old Duck: *(Old Duck enters the stage while Mother Duck is playing with the ducklings.)* Have all your eggs hatched, Mother Duck?

Mother Duck: One egg has not hatched but just look at all the others: aren't they the prettiest little ducklings you ever saw? *(They all stare at the egg that hasn't hatched.)*

Mother duck: I will have to sit on for a while longer. *(She goes back to sitting on her nest.)*

Old duck: Please yourself. *(Old Duck leaves the stage.)*

Storyteller 1: At last, the egg hatched and out came the little duckling. *(He says peep, peep and quack, quack very loudly.)*

Storyteller 2: He wasn't that little.

Ugly Duckling: Peep peep, quack, quack.

Ducklings: (*They all point at him.*) Look at him! He's so big and he's very ugly.

Storyteller 3: All the other little ducklings pointed and laughed at him.

Storyteller 3: The next day…

Mother Duck: Follow me ducklings, I'm going to teach you to swim. (*They all follow Mother Duck in a row. The Ugly Duckling is last in the line.*)

Storyteller 1: They went to the river and they saw other ducks and they began to laugh at the ugly duckling.

Duck 1: Here comes another brood.

Duck 2: As if there aren't enough of us already.

Duck 3: That last duck sure is ugly.

Duck 4: We don't want him here. (*They surround him and start to poke him.*)

Mother Duck: Let him alone. (*She pushes the other ducks off him.*) He was just in his egg too long and came out a little funny.

Storyteller 2: It wasn't just the ducks that made fun of him, the other animals did too. (*The turkey and chickens all surround the ugly duckling.*)

Turkey: He is too big.

Chicken 1: He is so ugly.

Chickens: He looks scary. (*Chicken 1 starts to peck him and leaves the stage; the ugly duckling starts to run and bumps into to two wild ducks.*)

Storyteller 3: The little duck was so scared he ran away.

Storyteller 1: Then he met two wild ducks.

Wild duck 1: What kind of a duck are you?

Wild duck 2: A really ugly one! (*They laugh and start to poke him.*)

(*Dog starts chasing the wild ducks and they run away.*)

Dog 1: What kind of a duck are you?

Dog 2: You are so ugly. (*The dogs run away looking scared.*)

Ugly Duckling: Even the dogs won't chase me as I'm really ugly.

Storyteller 2: He ran over the field and the meadow until he was cold and hungry.

Storyteller 2: He came to a little cottage. *(He knocks on the door and goes inside.)*

Storyteller 3: A tom cat and a little red hen lived in the cottage. *(They are sitting down by the fire.)*

Tom Cat: What do you want?

Ugly Duckling: I want somewhere to stay.

Red hen: You can't stay here, you are too ugly.

Tom Cat: Be on your way. *(They shoo the ugly duckling away.)*

Storyteller 1: Summer turned into autumn and the leaves in the forest turned to orange.

Storyteller 2: Winter came and so did the wind, rain and snow.

Storyteller 3: The ugly duckling was exhausted and fell asleep on the frozen river.

Ugly Duckling: I am so sad, I've no family, friends and I'm so ugly no one wants to be friends with me. *(The ugly duckling cries and falls asleep.)*

Storyteller 1: Winter turned to spring and some children came to the lake and started to throw bread at the duck.

Child 1: Look at the swans they are so beautiful.

Child 2: But the new one is the most beautiful of them all. He is so young and pretty. *(They point to the ugly duckling.)*

Ugly Duckling: Are they talking to me? *(He looks around and points to himself and he looks at his reflection in the water.)*

Ugly Duckling: I am beautiful! I never dreamed of such happiness as this while I was the ugly duckling.

The Boy Who Cried Wolf

Cast of Characters (26): Six storytellers, six sheep, six wolves, six townspeople, shepherd boy, his father.

(The shepherd boy is sitting on a chair centre stage; the sheep are all around him, grazing in the field. Townspeople and boy's father are stage left, miming working, and the wolves are stage right, asleep.)

Storyteller 1: Once upon a time, there was a young shepherd boy.

Storyteller 2: He lived in a lonely valley, next to a great, dark forest.

Storyteller 3: He had to look after his father's sheep and protect them from the wolves that lived in the forest.

Storyteller 4: It was a lonely job, and the boy was bored. *(Boy starts to yawn and stretch.)*

Storyteller 5: He wanted some fun and action.

Storyteller 6: One day …

Shepherd: Boy, oh boy! I'm so bored! There is nothing to do!

Sheep: Baa! Baa! Baa!

Sheep 1: Why are you so bored?

Sheep 2: Yes, you can play with us.

Sheep 3: We always have fun following each other.

Sheep 4: Don't you like us?

Shepherd Boy: Yes, but I'm bored. I want to be in the village playing with my friends!

Sheep 5: I have an idea if you want some excitement.

Shepherd Boy and other sheep: WHAT?

Sheep 5: Pretend there is a wolf attacking all the sheep.

Sheep 6: Don't listen to him. He *(points to sheep 5)* is always causing trouble.

Shepherd Boy: No, it is a brilliant plan. Let's do it right now. *(Boy goes stage left and shouts.)* Wolf! Wolf! Help! The mean, old wolf is coming. *(His father and townspeople run towards centre stage with shotguns, sticks and shovels as the sheep run off-stage.)*

Storyteller 1: His father and the townspeople came rushing to help him.

Father: Where's the wolf?

Townsperson 1: Where did he go?

Townsperson 2: I'll get him.

Townsperson 3: Did you see the wolf?

Townsperson 4: Did he go back to the forest?

Townsperson 5: Has he killed our sheep?

Shepherd Boy: False alarm! False alarm! I thought I saw the wolf, but it must have been a shadow.

Townsperson 6: False alarm. Let's go home. *(Exit father and the townspeople. The sheep return, laughing. The boy sits on his chair laughing and the sheep gather around him.)*

Storyteller 2: This excitement pleased the shepherd boy.

Storyteller 3: It made him laugh and clap his hands. *(Boy laughs and claps his hands.)*

Storyteller 4: A few days later, he tried the same trick again.

Storyteller 5: This time the sheep didn't know that it was a trick.

Shepherd Boy: Wolf! Wolf! The mean, old wolf is coming. *(Sheep scatter off-stage. Enter father and townspeople with shotguns, sticks and shovels.)*

Father: Good lad! Tell us where the wolf is!

Townspeople: Did he go this way or that way?

Townsperson 1: He won't get far.

Townsperson 2: We could follow his tracks.

Townsperson 3: But there aren't any paw prints.

Townsperson 4: Where's the wolf?

Shepherd Boy: False alarm! False alarm! I thought I saw the wolf. It must have been a shadow again.

Townspeople 5 & 6: False alarm! Let's go home again. *(Townspeople leave and the sheep come back, but this time they are relieved.)*

Sheep: YOU FRIGHTENED US.

Shepherd Boy: Hee! Hee! Hee!

Storyteller 6: The boy played the trick several more times. Then one day the shepherd boy thought he saw something big and furry moving in the woods. *(Boy looks towards the wolves but shakes his head and goes to sleep with the sheep. Wolves start slinking towards the centre of the stage.)*

Wolf 1: Have you seen this?

Wolf 2: What?

Wolf 3: Lots and lots of sheep.

Wolf 4: Where are they?

Wolf 5: Are you blind?

Wolf 6: Look over there! *(Points to the sheep and the boy who are all asleep.)*

Wolf 4: Oh, yes, now I see them.

Wolf 1: Sssh, be quiet.

Wolf 2: We could have a very good dinner tonight.

Wolf 3: You mean for the rest of week.

Wolf 5: The boy is by himself.

Wolf 6: Yes. No one is there to help him. Quick, let's go.

Shepherd Boy: I thought I saw something, but it is only a shadow. *(Yawns.)* I think I'll have another little nap. *(Wolves come to centre stage and prowl around dramatically, gesturing to the audience to be quiet. Then they grab a sheep each.)*

Wolves: We are mean, old wolves with a bad reputation. It's time to eat a juicy sheep for our dinner.

Sheep: Baa! Baa! Baa!

Storyteller 1: The shepherd boy woke up!

Shepherd Boy: AHHHH. Help! Wolf! Wolf! The mean, old wolves are here!

Storyteller 2: He called and called but no one came. *(His father and townspeople are stage left, miming working.)*

Storyteller 3: They were fed up with his lies.

Storyteller 4: The wolves took all the sheep.

Storyteller 5: The moral of the story is …

Storyteller 6: … nobody believes a liar, even when they are telling the truth.

Chinese New Year

Characters: Three narrators, three Jade Emperors, rat, cat, ox, tiger, rabbit, dragon, horse, snake, goat, rooster, monkey, dog and boar.

(Stage directions: three narrators on the left hand side of the stage. All the other characters walk around the stage showing confusion on their faces.)

Narrator 1: Long time ago in China. There was no such thing as time.

Narrator 2: Because there was no such thing as time, no one knew when to get up, or when to have their dinner or when to go to school or even when to play and have fun.

Narrator 3: Nobody did anything at the same time.

Narrator 1: The Jade Emperors who were the Emperors of Heaven knew this was a problem. *(The Jade Emperors are standing on chairs looking down on all the chaos.)*

Narrator 2: They decided to do some thing about it.

Jade Emperor 1: What are we going to do?

Jade Emperor 2: Everything is in chaos.

Jade Emperor 3: No one knows when to do things.

Jade Emperor 1: We have to come up with a way of measuring time.

Jade Emperor 2: Easier said then done.

Jade Emperor 3: How will we measure it?

Jade Emperor 1: Well, I have an idea.

Jade Emperor 2 and 3: Oh please, tell us.

Jade Emperor 1: Well, we could have a swimming race and the first twelve animals across the line will have a year named after them.

Jade Emperor 2: That's a wonderful idea. Let's call the animals.

Narrator 3: All the animals were summoned and were told about the Jade Emperor's solutions for creating time. *(They mime calling the animals and having a conversation while the narrators are talking.)*

Narrator 1: All the animals were excited and lined up.

Narrator 2: Both the cat and the rat knew they weren't good swimmers so they asked to Ox to help.

Rat: Ox can you help us, because you are so strong?

Cat: And so kind.

Ox: Of course, jump on my back and I'll help you get across the river.

(They all line up for the race and start swimming: the ox is in front with both the cat and rat on his back. They swim around for a while and just as they approach the end of the race the rat throws the cat off the ox's back and jumps onto the ox's back so he is the first to cross the line.)

Rat: I won! I won!

Jade Emperor 1: Well done. The first year in the zodiac will be known as the Year of Rat. *(He gets off his chair and shakes the rat's hand and gives him a medal.)*

Ox: You tricked me, rat.

Jade Emperor 2: Never mind, the second year of the zodiac will be called after you. *(He gets off his chair and shakes the ox's hand and gives him a medal.)*

Tiger: *(struggling to swim against the current.)* I am exhausted. I never swan so far before.

Emperor 3: The year of the tiger will be the third sign of the zodiac. *(He gets off his chair and shakes the tiger's hand and gives him a medal.)*

Rabbit: *(floating on a log)* I am sorry to say I can't swim. I hopped across on some stepping stones and then found a floating log which carried me to the shore.

Emperor 1: Well done, Rabbit. That showed imagination, so I am happy to name the fourth year after you. *(He gets off his chair and shakes the rabbit's hand and gives him a medal. Dragon comes swooping down.)*

Emperor 2: Dragon, why are you so late? You should have won as you can fly as well as swim.

Dragon: I was in the lead but then I saw the rabbit on a log and he needed some help so I huffed and puffed so that the log reached the shore.

Emperor 2: Well that was very kind of you and now you are here you will have the fifth year of the zodiac named after you. *(He gets off his chair and shakes the dragon's hand and gives him a medal.)*

Horse: Neigh! Neigh! I am going to be the sixth year. *(Horse comes galloping in with the snake next to him. Snake sneaks up behind and scares him.)*

Snake: Boo! *(Horse jumps back.)* No, Horse, I am going to be the sixth year of the zodiac.

Horse: Well, I suppose I'll have to settle for seventh place. I don't mind as seven is a lucky number. *(Emperors shake their hands and give them their medals.)*

Narrator 1: Not long afterwards a raft arrived carrying the goat, the monkey and the rooster.

Goat: We shared the raft that the rooster found.

Rooster: The monkey and goat helped me push the raft into the water.

Monkey: We worked really well together.

Emperor: I am very pleased you worked as a team. The goat can be the eighth zodiac animal, the monkey the ninth and the rooster the tenth. *(He shakes their hands and gives them medals.)*

Goat, Rooster Monkey: Hurrah, we can stay together on the calendar. *(The dog arrives very slowly.)*

Emperor 2: Dog, where have you been? You are the best swimmer out of all the animals.

Dog: The river was so clean I decided to have a bath.

Emperor 3: Well, as you are so late then you will have to settle for eleventh place. We have only one place left. *(He gets off his chair and shakes the dog's hand and gives him a medal. The boar comes along.)*

Emperor 1: Where have you been, boar? You nearly missed out on the last place.

Boar: It was such a lovely day I decided to stop and have a rest. I am here now and I am the final zodiac animal.

Emperor 2: Congratulations. *(He gets off his chair and shakes the boar's hand and gives him a medal. Cat struggles out of the water. He is not happy.)*

Emperor 3: I am sorry, cat, all the places are gone.

Cat: *(starts crying)* Boo, hoo. I will never forgive the rat.

Narrator 2: Since then cats have never been friends with rats.

(All the animals line up in order and take a bow. The cat is in the corner sulking.)

The Lonely Dragon

Characters: Three narrators, Daffy the Dragon, four birds, two crocodiles, two cheetahs, snake and frog.

(Stage directions: the three narrators are on the left hand side of the stage. Daffy is walking around the centre stage looking very sad with his head down.)

Narrator 1: Once upon a time there lived a Dragon called Daffy. He lived in a very big castle on the edge of a large cliff.

Narrator 2: Daffy was a very fierce-looking Dragon and he had huge wings and a very loud roar. He had no friends and used to spend his day playing by himself.

Narrator 3: He really wanted a friend. Sometimes while he was in the castle by himself at night he would get very frightened.

Daffy: Oh if only I had a friend to play games with I would be so happy. *(He looks directly at the audience.)*

Narrator 1: Daffy had a problem that meant that other animals didn't want to be his friend.

Narrator 2: He breathed fireballs whenever he felt lonely, sad, angry or frightened.

Daffy: I don't like being alone up in the castle by myself. *(He starts to huff and puff and breath fire balls.)*

Narrator 3: He was very sad and lonely and sometimes he would get angry too. *(Daffy stomps his feet.)*

Narrator 1: One day he decided that he would try to make some new friends.

Narrator 2: He flew off the edge of his cliff. He had never done this before so he was very scared. *(He takes his time jumping off the cliff and then he starts to fly by flapping his wings very quickly.)*

Narrator 3: He was flapping his wings up and down when all of a sudden he saw some birds.

Daffy: I see some birds. *(Birds flying around playing with each other.)* Mmmmm, I wonder if those birds will be my friends. I will go and ask them.

Bird 1: Look! What is that? *(points towards Daffy.)*

Bird 2: Is it a bird or is it a plane?

Bird 3: Oh no, it is that scary dragon! *(They all huddle together and they are shaking with fear.)*

Daffy: Birds, Birds, please be my friends. *(He gets down on his hands and knees and begs.)*

Birds: Oh no, we will not be friends with you.

Bird 4: Quick, everyone, fly away! We don't want to get caught up in his large fireballs, do we? *(They flap their wings and fly off.)*

Narrator 1: The Dragon was very sad but decided to keep flying to see if he could find some other animals who would be his friends.

Narrator 2: Then he looked down and he saw some crocodiles playing together by the river. He flew up to them and said…..

Daffy: Crocodiles, crocodiles, please will you be my friends?

Narrator 3: The crocodiles just looked at him and said…..

Crocodile 1: Oh no, we will not be your friends, you are too fierce.

Crocodile 2: Go away, you have fire breath.

Narrator 1: Daffy got upset and began to breathe fireballs. They were the biggest ones he had ever seen.

Narrator 2: The crocodiles jumped into the river and quickly swam away. *(They swim off down the river as fast as they can.)*

Daffy: I can't follow them because I can't swim. I feel so sad. I am going to cry. Oh look, there are some cheetahs.

Narrator 1: The cheetahs were in the jungle playing with each other. They were having such a good time. He flew towards them and said…..

Daffy: Cheetahs, cheetahs, please will you be my friends?

Cheetahs: Oh no, we will not be your friends, you are too mean-looking and you have nasty fire breath.

Narrator 1: Then Daffy began to breathe fireballs; they were even bigger than the ones before.

Narrator 2: The cheetahs were very scared and ran away. Daffy couldn't catch them because they were too fast. *(Cheetahs run away and Daffy runs after them but can't catch them. Daffy starts to pant because he is out of breath.)*

Narrator 3: Then he saw a snake. He said …..

Daffy: Please, Mr Snake, will you be my friend?

Snake: Hiss, hiss; why would I be your friend? You are horrible to look at and you have fire breath.

Narrator 1: Then he slithered up a tree. Daffy couldn't follow him because he didn't know how to climb a tree.

Narrator 2: The Dragon was very upset. No one wanted to be his friend.

Narrator 3: Night was coming and he was cold and hungry, he even began to miss his castle. He began to cry. Then he heard the sound of a Frog.

Frog: Ribbit, Ribbit, why are you crying Mr Dragon?

Daffy: I am alone in this forest and no one wants to be my friend.

Frog: Mr Dragon, I will be your friend.

Narrator 1: The Dragon stopped crying and became friends with the Frog.

Narrator 2: They played with each other every day and Daffy became very excited.

Narrator 3: Very soon after, he stopped breathing fireballs. He was very happy.

Narrator 1: He made lots of friends with the other animals in the forest including, the birds, the crocodiles, the cheetahs. He even made friends with grumpy Mr Snake. (*All the other animals come onto the stage and start playing with him and each other.*)

How Zebra Got His Stripes

Cast of Characters (20): 2 Narrators – can be jungle animals; 1 Zebra; 1 Eagle; 1 Elephant; 2 Giraffes; 1 Lion; 1 Leopard; 2 Gazelles; 2 Ostriches; 1 Peacock; 3 Monkeys; 2 Hyenas; 1 Rhinoceros.

(Stage Directions: Curtains open on all the animals in the jungle. They dance to animal-style music something like The Circle of Life or music from The Jungle Book.)

Narrator 1: Long ago, in the hot, dry grasslands of Africa's great Savannah, all of the animals lived, but they all had dull coats and looked the same. None of them looked distinctive. *(All the animals milling around the stage look the same, but their walks and body language makes them different.)*

Narrator 2: They would work together to collect food to last throughout the summer's drought.

Narrator 1: The only animals that didn't pull their weight in the Savannah were the lazy lion, the foolish rhinoceros and the extremely greedy zebra. These animals would sit around eating all day, their knobbly legs protruding from under their fat stomachs. *(Zebra, Rhino and Lion are sitting on the left side of stage, eating.)*

Narrator 2: The elephant, who was the noblest and wisest animal in all the animal kingdom, would sometimes scold Zebra and his friends. Leopard went with him. *(Elephant walks towards Zebra, Rhino and Lion.)*

Elephant: Zebra, don't you think you should help everyone else? We all must collect food and water so we will not starve in the hot summer.

Leopard: Yes, you know how hot it gets. Everything dies. We must make sure we have enough food to survive.

Lion: Oh, go away, Elephant and Leopard; we are hungry now.

Zebra: We want to eat what we want now. *(Points to a tree.)* Come on, Rhino, look, lovely lush green trees over there.

Rhino: Quick, hurry before those goody-two-shoes try to save some of it for the summer drought.

(Zebra and Rhino are laughing and joking and eating the leaves on the tree, while Lion sits in shade eating a big slab of meat.)

Giraffe 1: *(Puts his arm around Elephant.)* Do not take any notice of them, Elephant. They are not very nice animals. Rhino is foolish; Lion is lazy and Zebra is just … well, Zebra is just plain … grrrrrrrrrrrrreeeeeedy.

Leopard: Come on, Elephant and Giraffe, we don't need them. We can ask the other animals to help us. *(Eagle comes swooping on to the stage.)*

Eagle: Why do you look so glum, Elephant?

Giraffe 2: Hello, Eagle. We have asked Lion, Zebra and Rhino to help us to collect food for the winter, but they just want to stuff their faces now and not save any food.

Leopard: While we do all the work!

Eagle: Don't take any notice of them. I will help you because I can fly up into the sky and survey the hot plains and find the best food. Then we can all work together and get the food for the long, hot summer.

Elephant: What a splendid idea, Eagle. Giraffe, call the ostriches. Leopard, get the gazelles and I will get Peacock. *(Monkeys arrive on stage, swinging from the trees.)*

Monkeys: What about us? We want to help to collect the food.

Giraffe 1: Mmmmmmmmmm. Monkeys, you don't know how to behave yourselves. You can only help if you promise to do it properly.

Eagle: Yes, Monkeys, you can't be getting into mischief like you normally do.

Monkey 1: We promise.

Monkey 2: Oh, please, let us come.

Elephant: I don't know. Your mischief will delay us. *(Flashbacks to the tricks the monkeys played on the other animals in the jungle. For example, they could run away, knock on the ostriches as their heads are in the sand or scare the gazelles by pretending to be monsters. Ask for suggestions from the students. Let them come up with their own ideas. Act out the flashbacks. Make them as funny as you can.)*

Peacock: I haven't forgiven you, you know.

Ostriches: *(very angry)* Neither have we.

Elephant: Perhaps they deserve a second chance.

Gazelle 1: Well, leopards never change their spots.

Gazelle 2: *(Very meekly looks at Leopard who looks annoyed.)* No offence meant, Leopard.

Leopard: *(Looks annoyed.)* None taken. But I don't know why everybody says that because I don't have any spots.

Narrator 2: All the animals worked hard except for Lion, Rhino and Zebra.

(Lion, Zebra and Rhino are sunning themselves, eating, chatting, and playing. The animals mime working hard while Lion, Rhino and Zebra are sleeping, playing and eating. Music could be played while the animals are moving.)

Narrator 1: One stormy day in the heart of the African plains there was a rumbling in the Earth. *(Thunder sounds and the lights flick on and off.)*

Narrator 2: Then all of a sudden a huge cave appeared in the ground.

Giraffe: What was all that noise?

Gazelle 1: I don't know, but it was very scary.

Gazelle 2: *(Both the gazelles are in a huddle.)* Look over there.

Hyenas: *(Laughing nervously.)* Everyone needs to be careful.

Ostrich 1: I am not staying here.

Ostrich 2: Me neither. *(They bury their heads.)*

Narrator 1: A few animals crept cautiously up to this new and wonderful sight, and when Leopard, who was the bravest of them all, peered into the darkness, he saw something glittering.

Leopard: There is a big hole and there is something glittering inside it.

Monkeys: Come quickly, let's have a look.

Peacock: No, we have to be careful. We must wait for Elephant to see if he knows anything about this wonderful sight. Besides, I don't want to get myself dirty.

Narrator 1: Just then they heard the thunderous plodding of the elephant.

Leopard: Elephant, come and have look at this. What do you think it is?

Elephant: I'm not sure, but I will go ask my friend Eagle. Eagle knows all the secrets of the African Plains. You stay here. Don't move a muscle, and I will try to find Eagle. *(All the animals freeze or the curtain closes. Elephant and Eagle appear on-stage, entering from either side, and stand in front of the curtain.)*

Elephant: Eagle, what is going on here? Do you know what is happening?

(Eagle whispers something into Elephant's ear. Eagle leaves and Elephant calls the other animals.)

Elephant: Leopard! Giraffe! Ostriches! Peacock! Monkeys! Hyenas! Come quickly everyone. Gazelles! Zebra! Lion! Rhino! *(The animals come in from the back of the auditorium, except for Zebra, Lion and Rhino. The rest of the animals greet the audience, waving and smiling at them.)*

Peacock: Well Elephant, what is the story?

Elephant: There are all kinds of materials in the cave which you may choose from. You will be issued needles by the Ostriches so that you can sew your beautiful new coats, but there is only one needle each so take good care of it.

Ostrich 1: Roll up, roll up, get your needles here.

Ostrich 2: Only one for each animal. Lose them at your peril. *(All the animals line-up and receive their needles.)*

Elephant: Now you may go in, but there is to be no pushing and shoving. Keep in an orderly line.

Gazelles: Everyone is here except for Lion, Rhino and greedy Zebra.

Peacock: They don't want to come. They are too busy munching on the grass and playing. If they don't come, there will be more for us.

Elephant: Let them be. Come, hurry up. You are going to miss out.

(While the curtain is closed the stage hands create an illusion of a cave by spreading different types of material and props such as horns for the Rhino. The animals all go into the cave as the curtains open.)

Narrator 1: The animals were amazed. The cave was full of furs and skins, all glossy and new.

(All the animals are in the cave except for Rhino, Lion and Zebra, who are now grazing stage right.)

Narrator 2: Inside the cave, there were horns and tails of countless shapes and sizes, and lots of threads of a thousand different colours.

Narrator 1: The news spread far and wide and soon all the animals were on their way to see the cave, running and jumping, sliding and swinging, and slithering through the trees.

(The animals enter the cave one-by-one, every few seconds – the Monkeys, Hyenas and so on. Eventually Lion arrives at the cave, and he is followed by Rhino, who looks on rather sheepishly.)

Elephant: Where is greedy Zebra?

Rhino: He didn't want to come. He said there was lots of time to go visiting the cave.

Lion: He is too busy stuffing grass into his bulging mouth. *(Hyenas laugh. The Monkeys jump around, doing impressions of a fat zebra. Music plays and all the animals admire themselves and help put things on each other. Everyone focuses on Peacock. Music fades out and curtain closes and Zebra is lying on the stage steps, half asleep and munching grass.)*

Zebra: All those silly animals are gone to see the cave. I don't care as there is more food for me. Yummy, yummy! *(One-by-one the animals come out from behind the curtains. Zebra becomes more and more amazed as the animals get more and more spectacular until it culminates in Peacock or whoever has the most colourful costume. It is like a catwalk in a fashion show. The narrators can describe what everyone is wearing, as the animals walk up the centre of the theatre and back down and pose for a few seconds. They walk back up on the stage and behind the curtains which are still closed. Zebra is amazed by all this, and when the fashion show is finished, he talks to the audience.)*

Zebra: I am going to be the most beautiful animal in the jungle. I shall have spots like Leopard, beautiful feathers like Peacock and a gorgeous mane like Lion. I will be the finest-looking animal in Africa. *(Asks the audience which animal they prefer and what sort of things they would like to see him wear. Curtains open and only Rhino and Elephant are on the stage.)*

Elephant: Rhino, there is only grey left because it took you so long to choose. But here, have a horn. *(Rhino puts on the horn but puts it on wrong.)*

Rhino: I put the horn on wrong.

Elephant: I will help you to straighten it. *(Struggles to help him.)* No, there is nothing I can do.

Rhino: I suppose I will have to live with the horn.

Elephant: Oh, stop complaining. At least you have a horn; I am just left the grey material.

Zebra: *(Climbs onto the stage.)* I have come to deck myself out in wonderful colours and furs.

Elephant: There is nothing left.

Rhino: I got the last of the horns.

Elephant: There may be a few bits of black material over there, but to be honest, I think you are too late. *(Elephant and Rhino leave the stage.)*

Narrator 1: Zebra searched desperately and found some black material.

Zebra: It is a bit tight, but I can squeeze in to it. What do you think? *(Asks the audience what they think.)*

Narrator 2: Zebra pushed and grunted, oohed and aahed and finally he managed to squeeze himself into the black cloth.

Narrator 1: But it was a tight fit. It was bursting at the seams, especially around his fat tummy.

Zebra: I feel a bit peckish. I think I will stroll down to the stream to take a quick bite of a leafy bush.

Narrator 2: When suddenly, pop, pop, pop! His tubby tummy squeezed through the seams. *(All the animals come in and laugh at him.)*

Eagle: To this day his chubby stomach shines through his coat because he is so …

GRRRRRRRRRRRRRRREEEEEEEEEEEEEEEDDDDDDDDY!

The Selfish Giant

Cast of Characters (23): The Selfish Giant; The Cornish Ogre; 3 parts of the wall – Sad, Lazy and Frightened; 2 Trees; Ice; Frost; Snow; Wind; Narrator/Old man; 8 Children – Anna/Billy/Cathy/Ger/Dick/Ellie/ Fred/Harry; 2 grandchildren.

(Stage Directions: curtains are closed. The opening scene is an old man sitting with his two grandchildren grouped around him, sitting downstage left. Selfish Giant and Cornish Ogre are sitting centre stage, miming drinking tea and talking.)

Narrator/Old man: Children come over here and I will tell you the story of a giant that lived a long time ago. He had a lovely, beautiful garden with soft, green grass. There were the most amazing flowers and twelve fabulous peach trees. However, the giant was very selfish, and he shared his garden with no one.

Old Man: He used to say...

Selfish Giant: My own garden is my own garden and no one else can use it!

Old Man: The giant had been to visit his friend the Cornish Ogre and stayed seven years. *(Giant and Ogre drink tea and mime having a conversation.)*

Selfish Giant: I have been here for seven years, and we have run out of things to talk about.

Cornish Ogre: Yes, you have been here a long time, so maybe it is time you went back to your beautiful, empty garden.

Old Man: They said goodbye and the Selfish Giant returned home. *(Giant waves goodbye and they both leave the stage, going in different directions.)*

Old Man: However, what the Selfish Giant didn't know was that his garden was being used by the local school children. *(School bell rings. Eight children run up the centre aisle and start to play with the children in the audience. They run down the side aisles and reach the steps to the stage. The curtains open and there is a wall, centre stage, with three parts to it: there is the happy part of the wall; a frightened part of the wall; and a lazy part of the wall. The lazy part is in the centre. There are also two trees on each side of the stage: centre stage left and centre stage right. The children squeeze through a hole in the wall.)*

Anna: Right, I've got through! Come on, Cathy. I'll give you a hand. Mind the nettles.

Billy: Ouch! Take care, Cathy, the nettles are very bad today. Watch out.

Cathy: All right. Nearly, through. *(She pushes her way in.)* That's it. Here at last. *(Sighing)* Wonderful! *(Children chat as four more go through the hole, one-by-one.)*

Dick: *(The last one trying to get through and having difficulty.)* This hole seems to be getting smaller and smaller, unless it's my imagination.

Ellie: No, you've got that wrong, Dick. You're getting fatter. It's all that fast food you eat. *(Children all laugh and pull Dick through the hole.)*

Ger: I love this place so much, and I am so happy when we are all in here playing. *(Everyone agrees by nodding their heads.)*

Harry: It's seven years since the giant was here. I know it's his garden, but he can't come back after all this time, can he?

Fred: I hope not. But just in case we'd better make the most of it while we've got it. *(Children go off-stage. Lights focus on the three parts of the wall.)*

Frightened: Wake up, Lazy. If the Selfish Giant comes back, we will be in trouble.

Lazy: The giant hasn't been here for seven years. I am tired of holding up the centre of the wall.

Happy: I love seeing all the children playing in the garden. I am so happy when they come into the garden, but, Lazy, I think you should wake-up.

Lazy: I am going back to sleep. *(Starts snoring.)*

Frightened: I'm scared. I have a bad feeling.

Happy: You are always scared. Try to cheer up and be happy that the sun is shining and the children are having such a good time playing in the garden.

Tree 1: Lazy needs to wake-up.

Tree 2: Why don't we ask the audience to help us?

Tree 1: That's a good idea. When we count to three, everyone must say, "Wake-up, Lazy."

Happy, Frightened and the trees: One, two, three audience, everybody together – wake-up, Lazy. *(Eight Children come back on the stage and the trees and the two parts of the wall freeze.)*

Fred: Let's play a game of stuck in the mud!

Ger: No, that's really boring.

Ellie: I know! Let's play Giant's footsteps.

Billy: That's not funny.

Dick: What about blind man's bluff?

All: Oh yes!

Cathy: Here's my tie. Come on, Fred. Ready for the blindfold?

Fred: I'm not doing it.

Anna: You are a scaredy-cat.

All except Fred and Harry: Scaredy-cat; scaredy-cat.

Harry: Leave him alone, I will do it. *(Harry is blindfolded and the game begins. They run around having fun. There is the sound of footsteps.)*

Tree 1: Did you hear that?

Tree 2: Hear what?

Frightened: I hear it too. Wake up, Lazy.

Lazy: I'm sleeping. *(Giant enters while the children are playing.)*

Happy: Lazy, I think you need to wake up. NOW!

(All the children see the giant and they begin to squirm and then all run away.)

Giant: How on earth did those horrible children get inside my garden?

(Looks at the wall and sees Lazy only half-standing up.)

Giant: I see where the problem is. Lazy, wake-up now! *(Lazy jumps up and stands at attention.)*

Frightened: *(whispers)* I told you he was going to come back.

Giant: Wall, if you don't stand up properly, I am going to knock you down and build a new, stronger wall. This is my garden and NO ONE is allowed in here. I know what I'm going to do. I'm going to put up a sign. *(Giant gets a sign and puts it around Lazy's neck.)*

Giant: *(Shouts at the children.)* Can you read this sign, you horrible children?

Children: Trespassers will be presecutED.

Giant: No, you ignorant children. It is TRESPASSERS will be PROSECUTED.

Lazy: What does that mean?

Happy: It means anyone will be in trouble if they come into the garden.

(Giant exits, muttering. Curtains close to change the scene.)

Narrator/Old Man: Now the children had nowhere to play. *(Curtains open: the stage has changed, as the trees are now behind the wall and they are all upstage to give the illusion that the children are outside the garden.)*

Anna: Why does the giant have to be so mean?

Billy: We have nowhere to play now.

Cathy: We weren't doing him any harm.

Dick: Where will we play now?

Ellie: The road!

Fred: We could get knocked down.

Ger: We have no choice now. *(The children look forlorn and play with their heads down. They all look toward the garden.)*

Harry: How happy we were there! *(The children slowly walk off the stage.)*

Narrator/Old Man: Then spring came over the country. There were flowers blooming, trees in blossom and birds singing. Only in the garden of the selfish giant it was still winter. The birds did not care to sing in it as there were no children. And the flowers had no heart to bloom.

Ice: Well, Frost, I think our work has been done here.

Frost: I'm looking forward to having a break. *(Ice suddenly notices the sign: 'Trespassers will be prosecuted.')*

Ice: Look at this.

Frost: That Selfish Giant won't share his garden.

Ice: I know. Let's stay here until the Selfish Giant learns to share his beautiful garden.

Frost: I know, I will call Wind and Snow and get them to come and help. (*Takes out mobile phone and rings them. Wind shows up immediately.*)

Wind: What's the big emergency? I was very busy in Florida. It is hurricane season, you know.

Ice: Wait until Snow gets here and we will tell you all about it. (*A few seconds late Snow arrives on-stage.*)

Snow: I'm here.

Wind: What took you so long?

Snow: I was in Lapland helping Santa. What's the big emergency?

Frost: Anyway, look at this sign. The Selfish Giant won't share his garden, so we are going to stay here until he changes his mind. (*Ice, Frost, Wind and Snow freeze. Giant enters stage left, looking sad.*)

Narrator/Old Man: The giant was very sad. A year passed and he began to realise he was very selfish. One day he saw one of the children under a tree crying and he went to help him. (*Giant mimes seeing the child. Nobody else can see him.*)

Giant: Please, let me help. (*He reaches under the tree and mimes lifting up a child*) I have been a very selfish giant. I will open my garden up to everyone. (*He takes down the sign and exits.*)

Ice: Frost, I think he has learned his lesson.

Frost: It's time to go. I heard there is an ogre in Cornwall who hasn't been very nice.

Ice: Wind and Snow, come on. It is time to go.

Snow: Do you have a map?

Frost: No! But I have my new Sat Nav.

Ice: Come on, let's go! (*They leave the stage. One of the children spies a hole in the wall and climbs through. He calls the others.*)

Fred: I can't believe we are inside the garden again!

Dick: It's spring time.

Billy: Winter has gone.

Cathy: And there's no notice. The giant's notice is gone!

Harry: And the garden is more beautiful than ever. (*The children hear the giant's footsteps and hide behind the trees. Giant comes on-stage and sees* *them. He waves them over. They are frightened but they move towards him slowly.)*

Giant: Now I would like to join your games, if you please!!!! *(Suddenly looking around.)* But where is your little friend?

Anna: What are you talking about, sir?

Billy: Do you mean Fred over there?

Fred: He doesn't mean me. He means Dick. *(He pushes Dick forward.)*

Dick: Did you want something *(stuttering nervously)* Mmmmmister … ssssir … Mmmister … Ffffriendly … Giant?

Giant: I want to know where the little boy is, the one that I lifted up into the branches of the tree.

Ellie: But we haven't been in the garden since you put the sign up. Well not until today.

Fred: Then we heard your footsteps.

Anna: So we hid by the wall. I'm sorry that we trespassed in your garden, Mr. Giant.

(All apologize, suddenly worried that the giant might become selfish again.)

Giant: Oh no, no, no. You don't need to say sorry. I am the one who is sorry. Please think of this garden as yours now. But I wish you could tell me where the little child lives. I am very fond of him because it is through him that I realised I had been selfish with my garden. No wonder spring never came!

Ger: But this is all of us. No one else came with us.

Billy: But we will ask around in school tomorrow, and see if we can find out about your little friend.

Giant: Oh, yes, please. Now I really must have my rest. My old bones ache from all the playing. You carry on playing.

(Giant sits on the side of the stage and the children continue to play in slow motion.)

Narrator/Old Man: The years passed but the children were never able to find out who the giant's little friend had been. The giant grew very, very old. He could no longer play, so he sat in a huge armchair and watched the children. They all feared he would die soon. *(Giant mimes seeing the small child and calls out to him. Only Giant can see the small child. The* *children all stop playing immediately when they hear Giant talking. They look around but they can't see anyone.)*

Giant: There he is! Come on, little friend. Where have you been? I've waited so long for you. Come and join in the fun. *(He hobbles towards the child.)* My goodness, how I've missed you! I had a feeling I might die before you came to see me again. *(Giant moves to hug the child, and then draws back in horror as he takes the child's hands and examines them.)*

Giant: Why, who has dared wound you? Tell me quickly, and I'll fetch my sword and kill him.

Small Child: *(Audience just hears the voice, they don't see small child; the voice can be done by the teacher or drama facilitator.)* No, these are the wounds of love.

Giant: *(Suddenly in awe.)* Who are you?

Small Child: Once you let me play in your garden. Today, you shall come with me to a very special garden called Paradise.

(Giant sinks slowly to the ground. The small child kneels beside the giant, makes him comfortable and comforts him. The children, aware Giant has died, sadly gather flowers and place them around him.)

The Land of the Trolls & Gargoyles

Cast of Characters (18): Jack, Sarah, Rover, 8 Gargoyles, Gargoyle Bob, 4 Trolls and 2 Friends.

(Stage Directions: there are cushions on the floor and a few chairs centre stage.)

Scene 1

(Jack comes in wearing a Superman outfit. He is chasing his dog, and starts tumbling and rolling around on the floor with him. His sister walks past him and raises her eyebrows up to heaven.)

Sarah: Jack, will you calm down? My friends are calling for me in a minute. I don't want them to see what a nutcase you are. No wonder Mum thinks you are naughty.

(Jack ignores her and continues playing with the dog. He thinks he is a dog as well.)

Sarah: *(Getting very annoyed.)* Jack! Jack! Will you please stop? You are giving me a headache.

Jack: *(Still ignoring his sister and growling.)* Come on, Rover, let's makes a big massive fortress in the sand pit.

Rover: *(Gets excited, jumps up and down.)* Woof! Woof!

(Jack and Rover play with some cushions. Then they make a castle with the cushions. Sarah is cleaning up and sweeping the floor.)

Sarah: Is there any chance of you helping me tidy up? Mum will be back from work soon, and she will be very tired. You know she has been working so hard because she is frightened she might lose her job. *(Jack ignores her and continues building the cushion castle.)*

Sarah: JACK! JACK! Are you listening to me?

(She sighs and gives up when the phone rings.)

Sarah: *(On the phone.)* Oh My God, she didn't … What did he say? … I didn't show him anything ….

Jack: Rover, that's the best castle we have ever made. Let's get some soldiers to play with.

Sarah: *(Still on the phone.)* I can't believe it … he is so cute …oh my god ….

Jack: Hey, Sarah! Do you want to see the most amazing castle ever?

Sarah: *(Stops phone conversation.)* Mmmmmmm, let me think … No! No! NO!

Jack: *(Looks dejectedly at Rover.)* What's wrong with her? We made it all by ourselves. *(Rubs Rover.)*

Rover: Woof! Woof! *(Doorbell rings and Sarah goes to answer it. Her two friends are there.)*

Sarah: Hi, Girls. *(They air kiss one another.)*

Friend 1: Are you ready to go out?

Sarah: Nearly. I just have to wait for my mother to come home. I've to look after that wild thing.

Jack: Hey, do you want to see the most amazing thing ever?

Friend 2: Oh yeah, like a twerp like you can show us the most amazing thing ever.

Friend 1: We have seen a lot you know. We are 14 but show us what's so AMAZING! MAD JACK!

(The three girls laugh.)

Friend 1: MAD JACK! That's a perfect name for him.

(Jack shows them his fort. They all laugh at him.)

Friend 2: So that's the most AMAZING thing ever. *(She knocks down his fort.)* You are such a loser, MAD JACK!

Friend 1: Yeah, Loser. *(Makes L sign and knocks down the rest of the fort. Jack looks like he is going to cry.)*

Sarah: *(looks out the window)* Finally – my mother's back from work. Come on then. *(The girls run off stage left.)* Hi Mum, bye, Mum. Yes, I promise I will be back at 9 o'clock.

Jack: *(Hugs Rover.)* Girls can be so mean sometimes. We are lucky we are boys. Look at our lovely fortress. *(Goes to the left of the stage and shouts out.)* Hi Mum, when's dinner? I'm starving … so is Rover.

Jack: Come on, Rover; let's play our favourite game – Gargoyles.

(Jack and Rover start going wild on the floor. They are tumbling and rolling around with each other.)

Jack: *(Shows his claws and growls.)* I'm going to eat you up.

Rover: Grrrrr. Woof!

(They are chasing each other around the stage when suddenly a very expensive ornament falls to the ground and breaks. Jack and Rover look shocked, and they stand still, with their mouths open. The stage goes black.)

End of Scene 1

Scene 2

(Front curtains are closed. Jack and the dog both come out to the front of the stage. Jack has been sent to his room.)

Jack: That was a very expensive ornament. We should have been more careful, Rover. We always get into trouble. We don't mean to be troublemakers, do we, Rover? *(Rover shakes his head.)* It's just that I love playing with you because you are my only friend. Mum is always working and Sarah has her own friends. Why does she want to be friends with those nasty girls anyway? *(Starts doing impressions of them.)* Oh My God, you are so cool! He loves me so much… You are such a loser, Jack… Loser! Loser! Loser! … Mad Jack is such a loser… *(Looks at the ornament).* Now we have been sent to bed without any dinner, Rover. We are stuck up here all night. We will be so bored. What can we do Rover? … I know, let's go where the Gargoyles are.

Rover: *(Looks confused.)* Woof!

Jack: Yes, all we need to do is jump into the wardrobe and go out the other side and then we will be in the Land of the Gargoyles.

Rover: *(Still looks confused.)* Woof! Woof!

Jack: Well, it worked for the children in The Lion, the Witch and the Wardrobe. They went through the wardrobe to get to Narnia. Why won't it work for us? Come on! Come on! Let's go on an amazing adventure.

(Jack turns and asks the audience.) Boys and girls, do you want to come with us through the wardrobe? *(He mimes going through the wardrobe.)*

End of Scene 2

Scene 3

(Curtains open. There is a boat centre stage made out of chairs, with a tree stage right. Jack and Rover see the boat. They jump in it and take off. They mime pulling up the mast and getting tangled in the ropes, but then they get the sail up. They go faster and faster. Play "Titanic" music. This can be a movement and mime sequence if there is no boat.)

Jack: Look, Rover, there is a beach and a huge jungle behind it.

Rover: I'm scared. I want to go home.

Jack: I thought you were a dog not a cat. Scaredy cat! Scaredy cat!

(They land on shore and get out. They are very cautious, especially Rover. They move to the right of the stage. They hear something coming, so they hide behind a tree. Three gargoyles come on from stage left. They are dancing and thrashing about – destroying everything in sight.)

Gargoyle 1: I'm bored. I want to go home.

Gargoyle 3: That's going to be difficult because you have managed to get us lost. Yet again!

Gargoyle 1: But I saw something. I promise I did. It was over there. *(Points stage left.)*

Gargoyle 2: You are always seeing things.

Gargoyle 1: Oh, be quiet. Look! Look! Over there. It is a boat. Someone has sailed to our island.

Gargoyle 2: I'm scared. Shouldn't we go home and tell the others?

Gargoyle 3: Sssssssssssssssssssshhhhhhhhhhhhhh

(He sneaks around looking under everything like trees and plants and then he finds both Rover and Jack. Rover starts crying.)

Rover: I think the monsters are going to eat us.

Jack: Don't be ridiculous. Just watch this.

(Jack runs, shouts and jumps up and down, trying to scare the gargoyles. When they see how little he is they start to circle Jack and Rover.)

Rover: Look, they are massive. Look at the size of their teeth.

Gargoyle 2: They are tiny. *(They peer down at Jack and Rover.)*

Gargoyle 3: We could eat them for lunch.

Gargoyle 1: I'm feeling a bit peckish.

Gargoyle 2: Shall we eat them then?

Rover: Please don't eat us!

Gargoyle 3: Yes, let's eat them.

Jack: Be still everyone.

(The gargoyles freeze.)

Jack: Don't anyone move!

Gargoyles: Why?

Jack: Because I am your King. I am King of the Gargoyles, and this is Rover my loyal servant. From now on you will listen to ME.

Gargoyles: *(They bend down on one knee.)* Oh yes, Master!

Gargoyle 1: Is he really the king?

Gargoyle 2: Yes he is.

Gargoyle 3: He is a bit too small to be the king, isn't he?

Gargoyle 1: Well, legend has it that the King of the Gargoyles would arrive here in a boat.

Gargoyle 2: Welcome, Your Majesty. Welcome to our humble abode.

Jack: Thank you.

Gargoyle 3: Come with us. We will take you to our gargoyle campsite, and you can meet some of the other gargoyles.

Jack: Take us to your people, and I will show you how to be real people.

(Exit stage left and curtains close.)
End of Scene 3

Scene 4

(Curtains open. They all arrive at the campsite of the gargoyles. All the other gargoyles come to greet them. They are bashing into each other and falling over.)

Gargoyle 1: Hey, everyone! Hail the KING of the GARGOYLES!!!

Gargoyle 2: Hail, oh King.

(Everyone bows. One gargoyle comes and gives Jack a crown and sceptre and places the crown on his head.)

Jack: Okay, everyone, let's party!

(Music comes on and everyone thrashes and rolls around the stage. This could be a dance where the audience can join in.)

Gargoyle 4: I'm so glad he's here.

Gargoyle 5: Yes, I am too.

Gargoyle 6: He looks a bit small to be King.

Gargoyle 7: He looks a bit small to help us with the trolls.

Gargoyle 4: So, King Jack, how are you going to protect us from the trolls?

Jack: Who are the trolls?

Gargoyle 5: They live on the other side of the island. They like to fight with us all the time.

Gargoyle 6: They want to defeat us so they can stop us making noise and having fun.

Gargoyle 7: Yes, they are such horrible monsters.   .

Rover: *(Whispers to Jack)* Now I'm scared. Can't we just get back into the boat and go home?

Jack: Don't be silly, Rover. We can defeat the trolls. We are the gargoyles!

(All the gargoyles cheer.)

Gargoyles: Three cheers for King Jack! Hip, hip hooray! Hip, hip hooray! Hip, hip hooray!

Jack: I have a wonderful idea. We will build an amazing fortress. It will be one of the most amazing fortresses you have ever seen. We will put a moat around it and no one will ever come and stop us from having fun. We can be gargoyles every day. We can have lots of tunnels in it, so that we can hide from the trolls.

Gargoyle 8: We need to call for Gog then?

Jack and Rover: Who is Gog?

Gargoyle 8: Why, Gog the Builder, of course.

(Get the audience to shout for Gog. Gog comes up from the audience. He is a gargoyle, but he has a toolkit around his waist.)

Gog: What's all the commotion about?

Gargoyle 1: King Jack wants us to build a fortress to keep the trolls out.

Gargoyle 2: Yes, and it's going to have a moat around it.

Gog: Okay then, we'd better get started.

(The gargoyles, Jack and Rover mime building a fortress.)
End of Scene 4

Scene 5

(Four trolls come on stage and stand at the front. They point at the audience and look angry. The gargoyles are at the back of the stage, miming building a fortress. The trolls start asking the audience where all the noise is coming from. They accuse the audience of making the noise.)

Troll 1: What's all this noise?

Troll 2: *(Points to the audience)* Look, it must be them.

Troll 3: *(Asks the audience.)* Is it you, boys and girls?

(Audience denies that they are making noise.)

Troll 1: I knew it couldn't be them. *(Points at the audience.)*

Troll 2: Yes, they are too small.

Troll 3: Well if it's not them it must be those horrible gargoyles.

Troll 4: They think they are great just because they have a new king.

Troll 1: How do you know that?

Troll 4: I read it in the Daily Gargoyle.

Troll 2: That old tabloid.

Troll 4: That King Jack looks a bit small though.

Troll 3: Yes, we will be able to defeat him easily.

(The trolls are hit by rolled up pieces of paper – hailstones.)

Troll 1: Ow! What was that?

Troll 2: Oh, stop complaining. You do nothing but complain! … Ow!

Troll 3: We are being pelted by snowballs!

Troll 4: Where are they coming from?

Troll 1: Look over there! From that fortress.

Trolls: Quick, run!

(They run off stage. All the gargoyles start laughing and also leave the stage.)

End of Scene 5

Scene 6

(The trolls enter from stage left. They look very tired.)

Troll 1: That was a close shave.

Troll 2: Those gruesome gargoyles.

Troll 3: *(Speaks to the audience.)* We don't like them do we boys and girls?

Troll 4: Let's hope we get a good night's sleep.

Troll 1: Boys and girls, you let us know if the gargoyles turn up.

(They all lie down and go to sleep. The gargoyles come up through the tunnels from below the stage. They put their fingers to their lips and make faces at the audience, asking the boys and girls to be quiet; then the gargoyles tickle the trolls and run away. They repeat this two more times.)

Trolls: Okay, we give up.

Troll 1: If we can't beat you, we will join you.

Gargoyle 1: All bow for His Majesty, King of the Gargoyles – King Jack.

(Trumpet blows and Jack enters with Rover by his side. All the gargoyles and trolls bow.)

Gargoyle 2: Boys and girls, you need to bow, too.

Jack: Well, Trolls, do you want to be gargoyles now?

Trolls: Oh yes, please.

Jack: *(He puts his sword on their shoulders, one-by-one.)* I now pronounce you a wild thing.

(Everyone cheers and music plays. Everyone goes off stage except Jack and Rover.)

Rover: That was amazing. I can't believe you pulled it off. You really are King of the Gargoyles now. This is a great place. We can have fun here every day.

(Jack doesn't say anything; he looks very sad.)

Rover: What's the matter, Jack?

Jack: I've had enough of this place. I want to go home – to my own house, my own bed, my own family.

Rover: Well, we could just hop on the boat and make our way home if that's what you really want to do.

Jack: There is the boat. Come on quickly.

(They both run off stage. Gargoyles come back on stages, with the trolls, all having a great time.)

Gargoyle 1: Where's King Jack?

Troll 1: Look! Look! Over there in the distance I see them in their boat.

Gargoyle and Trolls: Bye, King Jack. Bye, Rover. We will miss you.

Troll 3: So what are we going to play now?

(They all skip off-stage playing with one another.)
End of Scene 6

Scene 7

(Jack and Rover walk onto a dark stage.)

Jack: Oh, at last we are home.

(Rover wags his tail and gets excited.)

Jack: Someone is coming. Can you hear footsteps?

Rover: Woof!

(The door opens and Sarah comes in.)

Jack: Oh Sarah! I've missed you. Have you missed me?

Sarah: *(Looks confused.)* I've been out with my friends … but, yes, Twerp, I've missed you. Mum says come downstairs for a hot chocolate. All that rushing around must have made you thirsty. I think she wants a cuddle as well.

Jack: Okay. Come on, Rover, let's go. Geronimoooooooooooooooooo.

(Jack storms off stage.)

Sarah: *(Looks at the audience.)* Some things never change.

No Excuse

Cast of Characters (11): Four Children, Four Bullies, Victim, Mother, Father

(Stage Directions: the stage is set up with the four children sitting very close together centre stage, in four chairs which should be almost overlapping. Have two in front and two in back, but not directly behind the ones in front. As each child says their part, they can change positions, but at any given time, each should be in a different position, i.e. one standing, one sitting, one slouching, etc. The other action takes place stage left and stage right.)

Child 1: It wasn't supposed to end up like this. I mean, I didn't really mean for this to happen. In fact, if you really look at the situation, you'll see that it wasn't my fault at all. I wasn't even involved. There is this guy at my school. Kind of a weird guy. Doesn't quite fit in, if you know what I mean. He's the kind of guy that keeps to himself and does his own thing. I never bothered him. I never really thought all that much about him. He was just there. And I was doing my own thing.

Child 1 and 2: It wasn't really my fault at all.

Child 2: It wasn't my idea. I just went along with it because my friends were. They thought that it would be funny to mess with this one guy at school. They just thought that if they broke into his locker and stole his phone, we could all get a good laugh out of it. It wasn't a big deal at all. I didn't really even do anything,

(Narrators freeze. Stage left, four bullies are standing in front of a locker.)

Bully 1: Quick, hurry.

Bully 2: Come on, will you.

Bully 3: I am going as fast as I can.

Bully 4: Look, we got it.

Bully 1: Hmm, don't look now, but guess who is here.

Victim: What are you doing?

Bully 2: Stealing your phone. What are you going to do about it?

(Bully 3 pushes Victim to the ground.)

Bully 4: We are taking your phone and you are not to say anything.

(Four bullies and Victim freeze for a moment and then all walk quietly off-stage.)

Child 3: I don't know why children pick on me. I'm really not all that different. I just like to keep to myself. I don't feel like talking to a lot of children. I guess I'm kind of distracted when I'm at school. I have a lot of stuff going on at home, you know? And so I think about it a lot. It's hard to focus on everyone having fun when I've got so much stress at home. I'm not trying to be anti-social or anything. I just have a lot on my mind.

(Narrators freeze. Stage right, Father is sleeping in the corner with a bottle. Victim is watching telly. Mother comes into the room.)

Mother: Look at the state of him. How long has he been like that?

Victim: Since I got home from school.

Mother: Wake up, you silly fool.

Father: *(wakes and grunts)* Shut up, you stupid cow.

(They have a fight. Father starts to hit Mother, then everyone freezes. Father/Mother walk off-stage and Victim freezes.)

Child 4: I really hate my school, though. Children there are just so juvenile and unfocused. It really brings me down. I have a hard time focusing there, and I don't want to make trouble for myself.

(Child 4 moves stage right and stands beside Victim.)

Victim: Do you want to go into town after school? I don't want to go home.

Child 4: No offence. I'd like to, but I don't think I should be seen with you.

Victim: Why not?

Child 4: Because they might start on me then, and I really don't want that.

(Child 4 moves back to his chair, centre stage.)

Child 4: They just kept picking on him. Every day there is something new – new signs on his locker, new nicknames for him. They just never let up. I didn't think that it was my place to say anything. I mean, I wasn't involved. I don't even know him that well.

Child 3: I just need someone to listen to me. I don't want them to fix my problems or even tell me what to do. I just want someone to listen; someone to help me sort through everything that is in my head so that I don't have to carry it all alone. It's hard to be so alone all the time.

Child 2: So we put stuff in his locker, right? Like a dead mouse. And he didn't do anything about it. He doesn't get mad, doesn't fight back. It's as if he doesn't even notice that we did anything. Well, it gets all of the lads really mad because they wanted to get at least some kind of rise out of this kid. So they devise even crazier stuff to get at him. I didn't really think it was a good idea. I mean, this kid never did anything to any of us. But you can't just say something like that to your friends. I mean, they'd think I was afraid or something, and I didn't want that to happen. So I just let it go.

(Four children freeze centre stage.)

(Stage right: Victim opens his locker, sighs and throws the mouse in the bin and freezes. Four bullies are watching.)

Bully 1: What is his problem?

Bully 2: Dunno.

Bully 3: We just have to think of something better.

Bully 4: Like what?

(Four bullies freeze.)

Child 1: I figured that a leader would step in or something. If it got too bad, someone would do something. And so I didn't need to worry about it. I wasn't doing anything wrong, so I should just stay out of it. Besides, these guys wouldn't do anything too bad, right? I mean, they would stop before it got out of hand. It always stops before it gets out of hand.

Child 4: They are so out of hand at my school. Everyone swears all the time and all anyone can talk about is getting drunk. I don't do any of that stuff, of course. They have no excuse to be acting the way that they do.

Child 3: They just kept at me. I tried to ignore them, but they just kept on going. It was like the more that I ignored them the more they decided to pick on me.

(Narrators freeze and action moves stage right again.)

Victim: Why won't you just leave me alone? I just want to be left alone.

Bully 2: Oh, come on. You're such a stupid little boy. Why won't you fight like a man?

Victim: I don't want to fight you.

Bully 1: Why? Are you scared?

(Victim and four bullies go off-stage. Centre stage – Child 3 is now sitting down with his back to the audience, head down.)

Child 1 and 2: No one was supposed to get hurt.

Child 1: This wasn't supposed to happen. Someone was supposed to stop it. There is no way that this should have happened here. A leader should have stopped this.

Child 4: I knew that something like this would happen. I should have helped him, but I didn't. I was too concerned with not being bullied myself.

Child 1: My excuse is that someone else was going to stop all of this.

Child 2: My excuse is that it was only a laugh. Nobody was meant to get hurt.

Child 4: My excuse is that I had to look after myself.

Child 1/2/4: My excuse is …

(As this last line is said, Child 3 gets up and walks off-stage. Everyone else freezes.)

Caught in the Act

Characters: Peter, Mother, Tim and Ted.

(Stage directions: Peter walks into the room and looks around to make sure that no one is there. Then he starts searching books on the shelf, opens one of them and discovers 20 Euros. He stuffs it hastily into his pocket. He hears someone coming and hurries over to the table. No one comes so he takes a comic out of his school bag and starts to read it. He hears his mother coming in to the room and hides the comic under his books and returns to study.)

Mother: Oh you are here Peter what a good boy you are. Have you been studying all afternoon?

Peter: Of course mother.

Mother: Good boy, you really are such a good example for your two cousins. By the time their parents get back from holidays the boys may have learned to behave better.

Peter: Yes, mother, I do try to set them a good example.

Mother: I know you do, love. *(She sighs)* But they are so noisy and rough. Of course they take after their father. No one in our family ever behaved liked that. *(She hears noise of the boys coming and she sighs louder.)* Oh come in quietly, boys.

Tim: Hi, Auntie; Hi, swot. *(They throw their schoolbags on the ground and plonk themselves down on the sofa.)*

Ted: We got into this brilliant fight on the way home.

Mother: *(Puts her eyes to heaven in horror.)* Fight! Fight?

Ted: Yeah, you should have seen Tim, he really bloodied Charlie Smith's nose. Look, just like this! *(They start to reinact the scene and the boys roll around the floor.)*

Mother: Children, children, behave yourselves. Why can't you be more like Peter? He has been studying all afternoon. I'm sure your mother would be pleased if you were more like Peter. *(Peter is sitting at a desk studying and looking angelic.)*

Tim: No she wouldn't, she said he was a wimp.

Mother: I'm sure she did not.

Peter: I think I'll go to my bedroom and study for my maths test tomorrow. *(He gathers up all his books and leaves.)*

Mother: Yes, darling, run along.

Tim: Auntie, could we have a pet mouse? Roger Spillane in our class said he could get us one.

Mother: of course you can't keep a mouse. What next? Peter wouldn't like it at all.

Ted: Auntie, do let us….. please! (*They both get down on their hands and knees and plead.*)

Mother: No. Sit down now and eat your bowls of nice stew. (*They all sit at the table and Peter re-enters the stage.*) Now, Peter, sit here and eat your nice steak. You need it to build your strength.

Peter: Oh thank you, Mummy.

Mother: Ted, have you got some disgusting chewing gum in your mouth? Take it out now!

(*Ted puts the chewing gum under the table. Tim knocks over a glass. Ted jiggles Peter's arm and Peter drops his knife.*)

Mother: Has anyone seen my money. I put a 20 Euros up on the shelf a few minutes ago; I can't seem to find it. (*She starts looking around the room.*)

Peter: I'll help you, mummy.

Mother: Thank you, darling. Boys, are you sure you haven't seen it?

Boys: No, Auntie.

(*They start to look, turning books and cushions upside down and throwing paper on the floor.*)

Mother: Stop! Stop! Peter, did you see anyone near this bookcase?

Peter: Only the boys, Mother. When they came in they put their bags near there.

Mother: SO THEY DID! Boys, did you take the money? Tell the truth.

Boys: No, Auntie, of course we didn't.

Tim: We just put our bags down there.

Mother: Go upstairs and tidy your rooms and when you've finished your rooms go and tidy's Peter's and don't come down until I have decided what to do with you.

Peter: No, No, Mother, I'll go up and tidy my room. I'd prefer to.

Mother: No Peter you stay here and finish your dinner. I am so upset that I need you with me. I never thought the boys would do this. I know that they are wild but I never thought that they would steal. My own sister's children! Of course, they take after their father: I never did trust him. They will have to be sent home. I couldn't…

Ted and Tim: Auntie! Auntie! We've found your money. *(They come running back into the room holding up the twenty euros.)*

Tim: It was in Peter's room, in this comic.

Mother: Peter, what does this mean? *(She looks at Peter sternly and in disbelief.)*

Ted: I think it means that he is the thief.

Tim: Yes, Auntie, he stole it to try to get us into trouble.

Mother: Peter, is this true?

Peter: Welllllll I just sort of borrowed it.

Mother: Go to your room at once. What am I going to do? This is terrible. Of course I blame his father. He is not strict enough. He spoils him. What am I going to do?

Ted: *(Pulls his chewing gum out from under the table and offers it to his aunt.)* Have a suck of this chewing gum, Auntie, it will make you feel much better. Look, Tim is going to give you his pet spider to play with, aren't you, Tim? You'll like that. *(Tim offers his aunt his pet spider.)*

Tim: You'll like it. Our mother would be very upset, Auntie, if she knew you thought we were thieves. Wouldn't she, Ted?

Ted: Perhaps if we had a nice big steak every night it would help us forget how you wronged us.

Tim: And a large pizza all to ourselves.

Ted: Just write a note telling the teacher we were too sick to do out homework tonight – a twenty-four hour bug.

Tim: And I'll tell Roger Spillane that we can have a mouse each. Have a good suck on that and Ted will make you a nice cup of tea.

(Mother puts the chewing gum in her mouth and puts her head in her hands.)

Anne of Green Gables

Characters: Anne and Diana.

(Stage directions: Anne is setting the table getting ready for Diana's visit.)

Anne: Oh I do feel so grown up. It's the first time I've ever been allowed to entertain someone to tea on my own. *(She hears a knock on the door.)*

Diana: Yoo hoo! Anne, where are you?

Anne: Oh, Diana, do come in. Let me take your hat. Isn't this lovely. Marilla has gone to the Ladies Aid meeting and it is the first time I've ever been allowed to entertain anyone to tea on my own. Look, she has given us a bottle of her home made lemonade as a special treat.

Diana: What a spread!

Anne: Yes! Sit down, Diana, and have a glass of lemonade. I'm sure it is delicious. Marilla is famous throughout Avonlea for her homemade lemonade. *(They both sit down at the table.)*

Diana: *(Pours it into a glass.)* Have you started your story yet for Miss Stacy?

Anne: Oh yes, it's called The Jealous Rival: it is so sad I cried quarts writing it.

Diana: It's bound to win the prize unless Gilbert...........

Anne: Don't you mention that name to me, Diana. It is a name which will never be spoken in this house. Have some more lemonade.

Diana: You always write such nice stories Anne. I think I'll have just a little more lemonade. It's much nicer lemonade than my mother makes.

Anne: Well I told you Marilla makes the best lemonade in Avonlea. Diana, what's the matter?

Diana: Oh Anne, I feel so sick.

Anne: You'll be better soon having some more lemonade: it will make you feel better.

Diana: No I must go home. *(Diana gets up and staggers out the door clutching her stomach.)*

Anne: Diana, wait! Your hat….. *(Anne shouts after her.)*

Anne: Poor, poor Diana … I wonder what the matter can be. She has hardly had anything to eat: nothing except the lemonade. *(Lifts the bottle and reads it.)* Oh no! It's not lemonade, it's Marilla's home-made wine. Oh, Anne Shirley you've done it again: you've made Diana intoxicated.

At Doctor Crowne

Characters: Miss Burkett, Mrs Davis, Mrs Esmond, Fifi, Didi and Girl 1, Girl 2 and Doctor Crowne.

(Stage directions: Mrs Burkett, the surgery receptionist, is walking around the waiting room straightening up the magazines.)

Miss Burkett: I hope we won't be too busy today, Dr. Crowne gets so upset if he has to see too many patients. *(Mrs Davis enters the surgery.)*

Old Mrs. Davis: I want to see Dr Crowne. Is he in?

Miss Burkett: Yes, Mrs. Davis he is in

Mrs Davis: What did you say?

Miss Burkett: I said yes Mrs. Davis, he is in.

Mrs Davis: There is no need to shout. I can hear you. It's my eyes that are giving me trouble.

Miss Burkett: Take a seat please.

Mrs Davis: What did you say?

Miss Burkett: Oh sit down, sit down. *(Old Mrs Esmond comes in and goes up to Mrs Davis.)*

Old Mrs. Esmond: Is the doctor in, Miss Burkett?

Mrs Davis: What did you say?

Miss Burkett: Over here, over here.

Mrs Esmond: Oh there you are, Miss Burkett. Where have you been hiding yourself?

Miss Burkett: I wasn't hiding, I was here all the time.

Old Mrs Esmond: Oh yes you were. There is nothing wrong with my eyes. I'm here to speak to the doctor about hearing.

Miss Burkett: *(She is getting frustrated.)* Take a seat. Oh no not over there, over here.

Mrs Esmond: Oh stop fussing, Are you here about your eyes, Mrs Davis?

(Fifi and Didi come dressed very skimpily.)

Fifi: Hi, is old grumpy George here?

Miss Burkett: Excuse me!

Didi: She means the doc, love. Is he here?

Miss Burkett: Yes, please take a seat. *(They sit next to the two old women.)*

Mrs Davis: Disgraceful clothes!

Mrs Esmond: When I was young we didn't even go to bed in clothes like that.

Fifi: Hi ,old girls, you waiting for grumpy George too?

Didi: We saw a terrible robbery down at the shopping centre. A young masked girl with a knife held up a shop assistant and grabbed thousands of euros. It's disgraceful.

Mrs Davis: Dreadful!

Mrs Esmond: Terrible!

Fifi: I wish I'd the nerve. I'd get myself some new gear. That girl had cold *(cool?)* black clothes…..

Didi: …..or take a trip somewhere.

(The door opens and a girl dressed all in black comes in carrying a large bag. She has a handkerchief around her hand which is bleeding badly.)

Girl: Can I see the Doctor, please?

Miss Burkett: Take a seat.

Girl: I've been in an accident: I want to get my hand dressed.

Miss Burkett: Alright, go straight through. It's an emergency.

Girl: Will you mind my bag for me? Please don't let it out of your sight.

Fifi: Did you see her?

Didi: It's the thief from the shopping centre.

Mrs Davis: What!

Mrs Esmond: What!

Miss Burkett: Are you sure?

Fifi: Of course I'm sure, she is wearing the same cool, black clothes…..

Didi: …..and carrying the same bag.

Fifi: And her hand is bleeding!

Didi: And I bet she's got a gun.

Fifi: I'm sure!

Didi: So am I.

Miss Burkett: What shall I do?

Mrs Davis: Try her coat.

Mrs Esmond: Look in her bag.

Miss Burkett: There's a gun in her pocket.

Fifi and Didi: The bag is full of money. Thousands and thousands of Euros.

Miss Burkett: What shall I do?

Fifi: Call the police.

Mrs Davis: Too late for that now, here she comes.

Mrs Esmond: Come on, Davis, we'll handle this.

(They knock the girl to the ground and sit on her.)

Mrs Davis: That will teach her to rob shopping centres.

Girl: what are you talking about?

Mrs Esmond: All that money in your bag.

Fifi: Yeah, we saw you in a mask and you had a knife and a gun and there's your coat.

Girl: Of course there is. I'm a security guard at the sports centre. I was bringing some money from there to the bank when I cut my finger.

Miss Burkett: What have we done? Oh, what have we done? Take a seat. Take a seat. I'll get the doctor. Are you alright?

Girl: *(groaning)* No, I think my arm's broken. I reckon I'm the only one *(person?)* who ever went to a doctor with a sore finger and came away with a broken hand. *(A second girl comes into the surgery.)*

Girl 2: Can I see the Doctor please? It's urgent.

Miss Burkett: Oh go in, go in. *(She doesn't take any notice of girl 2 because she is helping girl 1.)*

Girl 2: Thanks very much.

Miss Burkett: Now see here, you two hooligans, you got us into a right mess. You're delinquents, that's what you are. You should be locked up.

Girl 2: Thank you. Good bye. (*Girl 2 runs out the door.*)

Dr Crowne: Stop that girl! Stop that girl! She has just hit me over the head with a gun and stolen all my money.

Mrs Esmond: Come, Mrs Davis, let's go after her and we will see what you are made of.

Mrs Davis: Right. (*They both hobble after the girl.*)

Miss Burkett: What will we do? What will do?

Dr Crowne: I feel faint. (*He faints.*)

Fifi: Get old grumpy George a glass of whiskey, Didi.

Girl 1: This is a madhouse. In future I'll just go to outpatients in the hospital. (*She leaves, shaking her head.*)

A Winter's Night

Characters: Brian, Alice, David, Frank, Anne, George and policeman.

Alice: It's a very stormy night tonight.

Brian: It's cold tonight as well.

Alice: I'm scared of the storm. It makes such a frightening dinging noise.

David: Oh it's going to be a very bad night. I'm frozen.

Alice: Have your tea. You'll feel better then. *(They sit down to the table and Frank comes in.)*

Frank: I'm glad to be inside tonight. Any tea going, Alice?

Alice: Yes sit down and get warm.

Brian: The wind is really howling tonight.

Frank: It is quite scary. What's that? *(They hear knocking.)*

David: It's someone at the door. Get it, Alice. *(Alice answers the door.)*

Alice: Oh! Hello, Anne. It's a bad night to be out.

Anne: Yes and I'm very scared. There's a murderer escaped from prison. I heard it on the news and I didn't want to be in my house by myself. You don't mind if I stay the night do you?

Alice: Of course not, come in.

Frank: Don't forget to bar the windows to night, Alice, and lock all the doors. *(Alice and David mime locking all the doors and windows.)*

Anne: Well, I was very frightened coming here. *(She hears a noise.)* Oh my goodness, what's that?

Frank: Someone is at the door, again.

All: You go, Alice.

Alice: All right since none of you are brave enough. Hello, who are you?

George: Hi, I'm George. My car broke down and I got lost on the hills and I hear on the radio that there is a murderer escaped from prison.

Alice: Oh come in, come in.

David: Oh yes, there is a murderer at large.

George: Thanks for letting me in. I wouldn't like to be out there on the hills with a murderer on the loose.

Anne: Oh no, you are right I'm scared too. I came here for safety.

Alice: Have some tea, George. It will warm you up. (*George sits down at the table and starts to drink tea and warm up.*)

George: Good idea. Thank you very much.

Frank: What about a game of cards to pass the time?

George: Good idea.

(*They play cards and the time passes. Suddenly there is a loud knock on the door.*)

All: Alice, the door.

Alice: No. it's too late. I'm terrified.

George: I'll get it, Alice. (*George opens the door, and, as the policeman comes in, George sneaks off stage.*)

Policeman: Now, now. I'm looking for the murderer. He was seen coming into the house.

Alice: There's no one here but us playing cards.

Frank: And George.

Anne: Where is George?

All: He's gone.

Policeman: (*Shows them a mugshot.*) Is that him?

All: (*nodding heads*) Yes!

Policeman: That was him! We will get him, don't worry. (*Policeman leaves in a hurry.*)

Alice: We've locked the doors and barred the windows and huddled in here and then spent the night playing cards with the MURDERER! (*They all look around in disbelief and shock.*)

Printed in Great Britain
by Amazon

13987263R00048